BASICS OF INVENTORY MANAGEMENT
From Warehouse to Distribution Center

J. David Viale

A FIFTY-MINUTE™ SERIES BOOK

D1377643

CRISP PUBLICATIONS, INC.
Menlo Park, California

BASICS OF INVENTORY MANAGEMENT
From Warehouse to Distribution Center

J. David Viale

CREDITS
Managing Editor: **Kathleen Barcos**
Editor: **Christopher Carrigan**
Typesetting: **ExecuStaff**
Artwork: **Ralph Mapson**

© 1996 by J. David Viale.
Printed in the United States of America by Bawden Printing Company.

www.crisplearning.com

Distribution to the U.S. Trade:

National Book Network, Inc.
4720 Boston Way
Lanham, MD 20706
1-800-462-6420

99 00 01 02   10 9 8 7 6 5 4 3

Library of Congress Catalog Card Number 96-83618
Viale, J. David
Basics of Inventory Management
ISBN 1-56052-361-1

This book is printed on recyclable paper with soy ink.

LEARNING OBJECTIVES FOR:

BASICS OF INVENTORY MANAGEMENT

The objectives for *Basics of Inventory Management* are listed below. They have been developed to guide you, the reader, to the core issues covered in this book.

Objectives

- ☐ 1) **To discuss inventory management policies and objectives.**

- ☐ 2) **To provide inventory management tools and techniques.**

- ☐ 3) **To review financial analysis of inventory management.**

Assessing Your Progress

In addition to the Learning Objectives, Crisp, Inc. has developed an **assessment** that covers the fundamental information presented in this book. A twenty-five item, multiple choice/true-false questionnaire allows the reader to evaluate his or her comprehension of the subject matter. An answer sheet with a chart matching the questions to the listed objectives is also available. To learn how to obtain a copy of this assessment please call: **1-800-442-7477** and ask to speak with a Customer Service Representative.

Assessments should not be used in any selection process.

ABOUT THE AUTHOR

J. David Viale is the founder and president of The Center for Manufacturing Education, an international education and training company.

Dave's career in education started as a high-school teacher; then he went on to teach at various colleges and universities.

His background includes management positions at Arthur Andersen, Hewlett-Packard, and Fairchild Semiconductor. He was a practicing CPA and is certified in production and inventory management (CPIM).

His diverse business and teaching background gives him a unique blend of theory, practicality and financial impact. With this diverse experience, he brings a cross-functional perspective to his classes, speeches, seminars and key executive presentations, which he delivers across the United States, Canada, Europe and the Far East.

He can be contacted at

Phone: 408–973–0309   Fax: 408–973–1592

TO THE READERS

Developing a cross-functional understanding will become a global competitive issue for "Information Age" workers.

As organizations continue to flatten and decision making is assumed by individuals and team-based groups, "cross-functional smartness" will play a vital competitive role.

Cross-functional smartness is defined as the ability to quickly grasp new information and data regarding different functional areas and use it effectively in decision-making situations.

The level of cross-functional smartness will be impacted primarily by how quickly you, your peers, suppliers and customers can acquire an understanding of other functional areas.

This book is intended to give you an in-depth understanding of one of the major business issues facing companies today—inventory management.

With the mastery of this material, you will be well on your way to contributing to the globalization of inventory management concepts and subsequent waste reduction.

J. David Viale

WHAT'S IN IT FOR YOU PERSONALLY?

No matter how process oriented your organization is, there is always room for improvement. By using the information and tools presented in this book, you will

- Recognize potential conflicts among these areas. Although you may not have the expertise in each area to resolve differences or make decisions, you will know what key choices must be made in working out solutions.

- Develop a business perspective of inventory management and control.

- Enhance your professional portfolio of technical skills by mastering the major concepts, terms, definitions, tools and techniques that make up an inventory system.

- Understand how inventory management is applied in various manufacturing environments as well as distribution, wholesale and retail.

- Prepare for the nationally sponsored American Production and Inventory Control Society (APICS) examination.

CONTENTS

CONTENTS (continued)

INTRODUCTION

"Inventory is a very expensive asset that can be replaced with a less expensive asset called 'information.' In order to do this, the information must be timely, accurate, reliable, and consistent. When this happens, you carry less inventory, reduce cost and get products to customers faster."

"This book is intended to cover the tools and techniques in order to accomplish the above statement."

—J. David Viale

The world of business continues to change rapidly and dramatically. No longer will we see the stability of the past; reorganization is fast becoming standard. Business organizations are having to reinvent and reorganize themselves continually in order to meet demands of the global marketplace.

Everyone is faced with the challenge of developing the most highly educated and diverse workforce ever known. Because requirements for skill levels continue to increase, less-educated workers are struggling to find jobs. The competition for goods will only become more intense.

More important, this book challenges you to upgrade your existing skills and acquire new ones. Regardless of your present skill level, you have the opportunity to increase your knowledge of inventory management. Within these pages you will find

- An organizing question at the beginning of each module to orient your thinking—all content that follows provides the answer to the question

- Learning objectives that aid in measuring and understanding

- The distilled essence of inventory management theory and planning information

- Proven skill-building exercises for adding to your professionalism

M O D U L E

I

Inventory Objectives and Policies

Learning Objectives

After completing this module, you will be able to

- List the four objectives of inventory management
- Describe the major types of inventory
- List the major functions of inventory

WHAT IS INVENTORY MANAGEMENT?

The objective of inventory management is to replace a very expensive asset called "inventory" with a less-expensive asset called "information." In order to accomplish this objective, the information must be timely, accurate, reliable and consistent.

> Inventory management answers the question of how much inventory is needed to buffer against the fluctuations in forecast, customer demand and supplier deliveries.

Why Management Inventory?

The major reason for managing inventory is to reconcile the following potentially conflicting objectives:

> #1 Maximizing Customer Service
>
> #2 Maximizing Efficiency of Purchasing and Production
>
> #3 Minimizing Inventory Investment
>
> #4 Maximizing Profit

thus increasing return on inventory (ROI) and return on assets (ROA). These financial measures will be discussed in Modules III and IV.

THE FOUR OBJECTIVES OF INVENTORY MANAGEMENT

#1: Maximizing Customer Service

Inaccurate customer forecasts, a multitude of changes to the original customer orders, and an overall lack of account management are the major causes of poor customer-service performance in terms of on-time delivery—not suppliers, not purchasing. The result is excessive inventory, which ultimately leads to inventory write-offs and high product cost and lower profit margins.

In establishing the customer service level, determine how often you want to ship on time. One hundred percent of the time? Maybe yes, maybe no. Is 99.86% of the time good enough? (We will answer this in Module III.) However, let's simply consider the following points:

The more accurate the individual product-sales forecasting is, the smaller the forecast error, and the less inventory needs to be carried to maintain a specified level of customer service. By carrying less inventory, the capacity of machines required to build products is better utilized. Inventory is not built before it is needed, thus avoiding the mistake of committing capacity of machines too early. By carrying less inventory, generally less space is used, and it is not used too early.

There is a basic premise (principle) of this book that states, "the larger the forecast error, the higher the desired customer service level, the more inventory that must be carried." And we are not talking about inventory at the supplier, unless there is willingness to pay expenses such as storage, insurance and other related carrying costs. These costs are some of the major "hidden costs of manufacturing" contributing to the fact that many companies have increasing revenues and decreasing profits (and stock prices).

The solution to managing these costs is the establishment of an inventory model that will be discussed throughout this book.

#2: Maximizing the Efficiency of Purchasing and Production

There are instances when inventories are held due to cost efficiencies in procurement and production.

Goods may be purchased in greater quantities than are needed in order to achieve cost efficiencies in purchasing or transportation. When goods are purchased in this way, some inventory may result. However, agreements called "volume purchase orders" (blanket POs) may be established. These allow for increasing discounts as volumes increase and, at the same time, specify that deliveries take place as needed. This approach supports the Just-in-Time philosophy in Module IV.

In manufacturing, long production runs (large lot sizes) of a single product are usually much more efficient than short runs. Managers are often measured by the amount of product they produce, which acts as an incentive for longer production runs. Long runs result in inventory that sits for long periods of time. Theoretically, this inventory represents miscommitted capacity and a reduction in machine flexibility. Remember, if you can't ship the product, don't build it—no matter what the benefits of long runtime are.

#3: Minimizing Inventory Investment

Inventories tie up cash that the company could use elsewhere in the business. Excess inventory can create a negative cash flow, something that must be avoided. This is why the Financial people work to keep inventories as low as possible.

#4: Maximizing Profit

Profit can be maximized by increasing revenue or decreasing cost. One of the best ways to do this is by proper management of inventory.

HANDLING CONFLICTING OBJECTIVES

Meeting the objectives just discussed requires balancing short-term as well as the long-term objectives. Whether used to provide customer service or to achieve efficiencies in procurement or production, the need to carry inventories conflicts with management's desire to minimize inventory investment. Long production runs tend to create inventories; marketing people want stocks of a larger variety of products and options to serve a broad customer demand. High levels of inventory also take up space in factories and distribution centers, thus incurring additional cost of storage, insurance, etc.

Manufacturing, retailers, wholesalers, and even banks and hospitals are faced with balancing these objectives.

Reconciling these conflicting objectives is a primary goal of inventory management and the material presented in this book.

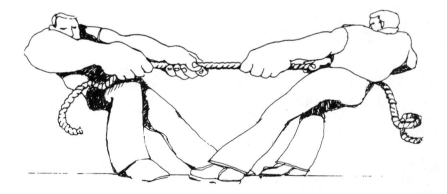

INVENTORY CATEGORIES

There are five basic types of inventory: *raw material, work-in-process, finished goods, distribution inventory* and *maintenance, repair, and operating (MRO) supplies.*

► Raw Material

This includes all the purchased parts and direct materials that go into the end product. This type of inventory has value added to it as it flows together as subassemblies, assemblies and finally into the shippable product.

► Work-in-Process

This is inventory in the process of being assembled into final products. Raw materials are released from inventory and moved to a work center. People (direct labor) and/or machines are used to add value by putting the parts together as subassemblies, assemblies and then into final products. These parts may be restocked temporarily until withdrawn for use later in the production process. While they are in this state, they may be referred to as *semifinished assemblies.*

► Finished Goods

These are shippable inventories ready to be delivered to distribution centers, retailers, wholesalers or directly to customers.

► Distribution Inventory

This is inventory held at points as close to the customer as possible. Distribution points, such as warehouses or stores, may be owned and operated by the manufacturer or may be independently owned and operated. However, managing inventories is necessary regardless of ownership, so the term "distribution centers" is used throughout this book to indicate intermediate storage locations, pending delivery to the final customer.

► Maintenance, Repair and Operating (MRO) Supplies

These items are held by most companies. These inventories are often low cost, and include office and operating supplies and services.

It is obvious, therefore, that all organizations—whether manufacturers, wholesalers, retailers, banks, hospitals or even the Federal Reserve—have some inventory concerns.

TYPES OF INVENTORY

Theoretically, there are two components of any inventory—*cycle stock* and *safety stock*.

1. *Cycle stock* is made up of the most "active" parts contained in the inventories (the high runners).

2. *Safety stock* (finished goods), also referred to as buffer stock, is used to protect against the fluctuations in demand or supply. It makes up inventory held to buffer against fluctuations in forecast, changes in a customers order, or late shipments from a supplier. The impact of safety stock in a manufacturing environment is to release an order and bring inventory in before it is really needed. In the master schedule, safety stock is maintained to protect against forecast error.

From a physical standpoint, these two types of inventory are not separated.

In addition to the types of inventory, inventory functions represent another way of looking at inventory. All of the following types of inventory act to buffer fluctuation in supply and demand. They add no value to the process and result in additional cost to carry, store, etc. However, they are necessary in order to ensure high levels of customer service. All types of businesses (retailers, manufacturers, banks) are challenged with the conflicting objectives of minimizing inventory and ensuring high levels of customer service.

Decoupling Inventory

This is a term used sometimes instead of *safety stock* to establish a buffer between product demand and product supply. It is used in work-in-process inventories. As factory work orders pass from machine to machine, queues (stocks) of inventory are often planned to enable each work center (machine) to absorb variations in workload due to such things as product mix changes. These queues of work separate the operations so that each work center can produce somewhat independently from other work centers. The objective is to prevent idle time in the factory of expensive, direct-labor people. Decoupling stock is used most often in build-to-order job shops. Job shops will be discussed in Module II under the discussion of manufacturing environments.

Transportation (Pipeline) Inventory

This can be simply thought of as inventory that is being moved from one location to another. Typically it is from the factory to a stocking-point distribution center as close to the end customer as possible. Pipeline inventories also represent the finished goods of the supplier. The time the inventory spends in the "pipeline" has an impact on the lead times and inventory levels. The components of this transportation time include order entry, shipping, transportation and receiving time at the destination.

Anticipation Stock

This includes finished goods, work-in-process and raw materials, and is usually applied to inventory buildups for a seasonal demand or planned shutdowns of a manufacturing plant.

Hedging Stock

This includes finished goods, work-in-process and raw materials and is similar to anticipation stock. Hedging stock is a form of inventory buildup but is done in anticipation of some event that may not actually come about. This differentiates it from anticipation stock. Hedging stocks may be established because of

- Pending labor strikes in the supplier base

- Predicted price increases for materials

- Political instability in countries where suppliers are located

- Long lead-time items

SUMMARY

This module described five basic types of inventory: raw materials, work-in-process, semifinished assemblies, finished goods, and MRO supplies. Objectives for inventory are identified as minimizing investment while still providing a high level of customer service, maximizing profit and providing for efficiencies in procurement and manufacturing. Certain aggregate concerns regarding inventory center on financial objectives and measures, such as return on investment (ROI) and inventory turnover.

Company strategy often uses inventory where products have seasonal demand or where hedging may be necessary to guard against anticipated supply disruptions.

In the next module we will look at the types of inventory information systems and how each works in the various types of manufacturing environments: build-to-order, build-to-stock, engineer-to-order and assemble-to-order.

EXERCISE 1: Match Game

Match the following descriptions with the appropriate terms. See page 111 in the back of the book for the answers.

_____ **1.** These inventories include janitorial supplies and services.

_____ **2.** Inventory that is carried to buffer against fluctuations in forecast sales.

_____ **3.** Time inventory spends in the "pipeline" that has an impact on the inventory levels, including time spent on order entry, shipping, transportation and receiving.

_____ **4.** This is part of the inventory that is actively used to build products.

_____ **5.** This inventory separates the operations so work centers can produce independently from each other, which prevents idle time.

_____ **6.** This inventory may be established because of pending labor strikes.

_____ **7.** Applies to inventory buildups before a seasonal busy period or planned shutdown.

a. decoupling inventory

b. anticipation inventory

c. safety stock

d. transportation inventory

e. maintenance, repair and operating supplies (MRO)

f. hedging stock

g. cycle stock

EXERCISE 2: Fill In the Blanks

Please complete the following exercise. See page 112 in the back of the book for the answers.

1. List the four objectives of inventory management.

    a. _____

    b. _____

    c. _____

    d. _____

2. List three major types of inventory.

    a. _____

    b. _____

    c. _____

M O D U L E

II

Independent Demand Inventory Systems

Learning Objectives

After completing this module, you will be able to

- Describe the four major types of manufacturing environments
- Define the three types of manufacturing processes
- Describe the major independent demand systems

INVENTORY INFORMATION SYSTEMS

In this module we will look at independent demand inventory information systems. Dependent demands models will be discussed in Module VI.

Before going any further, consider the following:

▶ The choice of the appropriate model and formula must be consistent with the overall business plan and objectives, and with the strategies for research and development (R&D), marketing, finance and manufacturing. The inventory system should be included in the manufacturing strategy, which primarily supports the marketing strategy and secondarily the R&D and finance strategies.

▶ The manufacturing environment that the inventory system will support must be taken into account. These manufacturing environments include build-to-stock, build-to-order, engineer-to-order, and assemble-to-order, and are discussed in this module.

▶ Nonmanufacturing environments (retailers, wholesalers, banks, hospitals, etc.) must also consider how inventory levels impact their business.

▶ The inventory information system has to fit the volume variety matrix discussed later in this module.

INDEPENDENT DEMAND SYSTEMS AHEAD

INDEPENDENT DEMAND MODELS

Independent demand models are methods to manage items whose demand is influenced by customer demand or demand from outside of the company control.

Independent demand systems are used to determine levels of finished goods inventory. This method is used by retail, wholesale and manufacturing companies. Even banks use this system to determine the level of paper stock to be carried to support the manufacture of checks and other legal documents. Hospitals must inventory medical supplies, bed linens, instruments, etc.; shelf lives in these situations have a major impact on inventory levels.

The *independent demand inventory system* has five different models or formulas.

> #1. Fixed Reorder CYCLE Inventory Model
>
> #2. Fixed Reorder QUANTITY Inventory Model
>
> #3. Optional Replenishment System
>
> #4. Joint Replenishment System
>
> #5. Forecasting (discussed in Module III)

Following is a discussion of each type of independent demand system.

#1. Fixed Reorder CYCLE Inventory Model

This independent demand model places a "fixed order quantity" on a predetermined time schedule (daily, weekly, etc.).

The actual order quantity will vary from order to order based on how many units have shipped. A maximum inventory level is established based on experience, budget or targeted inventory levels.

The order quantity will be the difference between what was used during the period and the maximum (targeted) inventory. For example, if 500 units are on hand and the maximum targeted inventory is 1500 units, the order quantity would be 1000 to replace the items shipped during the period.

#2. Fixed Reorder QUANTITY Inventory Model

A variation to the Fixed Reorder CYCLE Inventory Model is the Fixed Reorder QUANTITY Model. In this model a fixed quantity is established, usually using the economic order quantity (EOQ) formula described in Module III. This module uses a fixed quantity rather than the fixed time period described in the Fixed Reorder CYCLE method.

The fixed order quantity is placed every time the inventory reaches a pre-determined order point. This order point is set at a level whereby there is sufficient inventory to cover the demand from the time material is ordered from the supplier until it is received in the warehouse.

ROP = Reorder Point

DLT = Forecast Demand Through the Lead Time

SS = Safety Stock*

DMLT = Demand During Manufacturing Lead Time

ROP = DLT + SS

A variation to this formula is called the "double reorder point formula." This formula is used in determining order quantities in combined manufacturing and distribution environments.

The formula for double reorder point is shown below:

Order point 1 (OP_1) = DLT + SS

Order point 2 (OP_2) = OP_1 + DMLT

---

*The amount of safety stock carried for an inventory item in a periodic review system depends on the amount of variation in demand (aka forecast error) and the desired level of on-time shipments. (Safety stock calculation is covered in Module III.)

INDEPENDENT DEMAND MODELS
(continued)

Reorder Point with Safety Stock

The traditional "saw-tooth diagram" in Figure 2.1 graphically shows the reorder point formula.

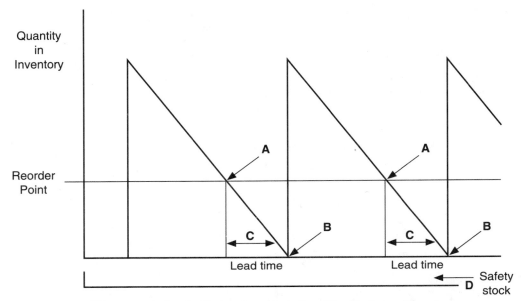

Figure 2.1: A Reorder Point with Safety Stock

A = Reorder Point—The point at which an order must be placed so it can be received before the inventory level gets to zero

B = Point at which a new order is received and the on-hand balance is increased by the order quantity

C = Lead time before the order is received

D = Safety stock carried to buffer against shortages and stockouts

In this system, inventory levels are reviewed periodically and all orders are placed at one time, often for all items in stock, to replenish the inventories up to some target level. This approach is applicable especially in retail businesses where goods are often ordered from a common source and where it is not feasible to keep perpetual inventory records. However, modern point-of-sale devices make possible perpetual inventory records for retailers in many situations today.

EXERCISE 1: Calculations

Using the following information about a regional warehouse that uses a double order point system, calculate the order points and reorder points. See page 111 in the back of the book for the answers.

Average weekly demand	2,000 units
Safety stock	200 units
Manufacturing lead time	3 weeks
Replenishment lead time	2.0 weeks

#3. Optional Replenishment System

This is a type of order point replenishment system where the minimum is the order point and the maximum is the level the inventory is not to exceed. The order quantity is variable and is calculated by subtracting the on-hand inventory from the maximum inventory, as the result falls below the minimum quantity. The min-max system is used commonly for low dollar volume items ("C" parts). It prevents ordering items in very small quantities. It is also useful when periods of low demand are anticipated or where it is desirable to use up current quantities of stock before replenishing, such as for items subject to spoilage or deterioration. The main advantage of this system is its simplicity.

#4. Joint Replenishment System

A joint order in purchasing is an order in which several items are combined to obtain volume or transportation discounts. Joint replenishment happens when items kept in the same inventory are ordered from one supplier. In production situations, it may be the case that multiple items are produced from a single work center or from a single major setup operation at a work station, with only minor setups needed for different items within a group. Some of the benefits achieved from joint replenishment in these situations are listed on the following page.

INDEPENDENT DEMAND MODELS (continued)

► *For purchased items:*

- Transportation economies

- Reduced order costs

- Discounts based on order value

- Accounting efficiencies achieved through reduction in paperwork

► *For manufactured items:*

- Minor, rather than major, setups

- Reduced setup time and cost

- Reduced paperwork

- More effective scheduling

Visual Review Systems

The visual review system (VRS) is completed by walking up and down aisles of inventory and visually scanning and, if necessary, counting on-hand inventory to determine reorder quantities.

A common VRS is the two-bin system. This method uses two storage locations with stock of the same item. When one location, or bin, becomes empty, a replenishment order is placed to refill it while material is being used from the second bin. This method is used frequently for low-value items that are stocked on the manufacturing floor.

Time-Phased Order Point (TPOP)

Time-phased order point is a technique that has been borrowed from Material Requirements Planning (MRP) logic as a means to determine when replenishment orders must be placed to ensure a continuous supply of goods. The logic of TPOP is illustrated in Module V.

ENVIRONMENTS AND THEIR EFFECTS ON INVENTORY MANAGEMENT

Business environments often determine the type of inventory control systems needed in various industries. Following is a brief overview of the major types of business environments and their impact on each type of inventory management consideration.

The Volume Variety Matrix below illustrates that when product variety increases, the product volume decreases. The chart on the following page expands on this.

Volume Variety Matrix

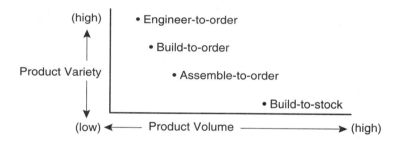

Review of Business Environments

Type of Business Environment	Description	Impact on Inventory
Engineer-to-order	• Requires unique one-of-a-kind engineering design • Unique bill of materials and part # • Work does not begin until customer specifications are complete • Very long lead time • One-of-a-kind products • Huge profit margin per unit	• No finished goods and little or no raw material until the customer specifications are complete
Build-to-order	• More products than engineer-to-order; however, volumes are very low • Customer lead times are long, but not as long as engineer-to-order • High profit margin per unit	• No finished goods • Raw material and work-in-process inventories • Safety stock carried for long lead time items
Assemble-to-order	• Fewer products than build-to-order, but volumes are higher • Build to forecasted options • Assemble option to customer specification • Use of planning bills • Medium profit margin per item	• Little if any finished goods • Inventory based on option forecast • Raw material held, especially for long lead time items
Build-to-stock	• Very low product variety, high product volume • Build to forecasted demand of independent items • Buffer for forecast error must be calculated • Low profit margin per item	• Inventory carried at the finished goods level • Emphasis on instant availability
Wholesale	• Buy from manufacturers and sell to retailers • Must vie for shelf and floor space • May do some repackaging • Provides services of bulk storing and quick delivery	• Primarily carry finished goods
Retail	• Emphasis on service and merchandising products provided by manufacturer • Provide space to display wide variety of products available to customer instantly	• Carry only finished goods
Others: Banks, insurance	• Provide service relating to checks and other legal documents	• Combination of preprinted form and assemble-to-order (checks) • Raw material (paper) held by printer
Hospital	• Service requires medical supplies, linens, etc.	• Linens and other medical supplies

ORDER CYCLES AND LEAD TIMES

The figure below shows how three major information systems tie in with the actual physical flow of goods.

Physical Flow

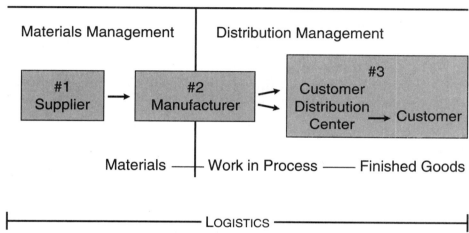

The three major information systems are customer order processing (customer orders), manufacturing order processing (work orders) and supplier order processing (purchase orders).

▶ **Customer Order Processing Time**

The customer order processing begins with order entry—either directly into the master schedule, or first through an order entry module that checks for order correctness, credit status, etc. and then into the master schedule.

▶ **Manufacturing Order Processing Time**

The customer orders, once entered into the master schedule, create manufacturing orders or purchase orders via the MRP system.

ORDER CYCLES AND LEAD TIMES (continued)

The time from the work order release until the order is complete makes up manufacturing lead time. This lead time varies based on the type of manufacturing. The major components of lead time are

- Queue (the time the inventory is sitting on the shop floor waiting to be worked on)

- Setup (time spent preparing the machine)

- Run time (time the machine is actually running)

- Wait (time spent waiting for the finished item at one machine to be moved to the next

- Move (time spent moving to the next machine)

- Finished goods inventory (time spent waiting to move to the end customer)

▶ **Purchasing Order Processing Time**

Purchasing order-processing lead time includes the time to get a purchase requisition, release it to the supplier and receive it into the warehouse or directly to the production floor.

▶ **Reconciling the Physical Flow with the Information Flow**

Reconciling the information flow (from MPS through MRP and on to the suppliers) with the physical flow of the parts from suppliers into manufacturing and then on to the customers is one of the major challenges in companies today.

In many cases, products can actually be built faster than orders can be entered and processed through the manufacturing and purchasing information systems. In meeting time-to-market objectives, information systems bottlenecks have taken the place of manufacturing (machine) bottlenecks.

This situation worsens when changes take place, especially customer changes. Marketing people, financial people and particularly executives have little appreciation for the time the entire process takes. It takes time to analyze and make corrections or changes, not just to the customer order, but all the way through manufacturing and the affected suppliers.

Additional time must be spent "coercing" the suppliers and "arm-twisting" the operations people to make the changes.

This situation causes a large number of part shortages and late deliveries, both from suppliers and to customers. In addition, costs such as premiums and expedited charges are incurred, which seldom get passed on to the customer.

The answer to this problem is twofold.

1. Good account management should point out to the customers the cost of the changes they are asking for.

2. A significant improvement in manufacturing software is needed, which will allow for instantaneous updates of all the information.

Summary

In the meantime, the physical flow and the information flow will continue to be reconciled through physical inventories and/or cycle counting (these concepts are covered in Module IV).

EXERCISE 2: *Choose the Correct Answer*

Choose the correct answer. See page 111 in the back of the book for the answers.

1. All of the following are major types of manufacturing environments EXCEPT:

    A. Build-to-order
    B. Build-to-stock
    C. Assemble-to-order
    D. Assemble-to-build

2. Which of the following systems would be best for determining the amount of component parts to be used in a product?

    A. Independent demand system
    B. MRP system
    C. Dependent demand system
    D. Both B and C

3. The use of reorder point systems is appropriate when

    A. There are many small orders.
    B. Lot sizes are fixed/known.
    C. Cost of stocking is high.
    D. All of the above

4. Which of the following would be best suited to an independent demand system?

    A. Build-to-order products
    B. Service parts
    C. Parts used in end items

5. The formula for calculating reorder point is

    A. $\dfrac{\text{Cost of sales}}{\text{Average inventory}}$
    B. DLT + S
    C. Safety stock + order quantity
    D. None of the above

6. Time-phased order point uses the same logic as

    A. MRP
    B. Exponential smoothing
    C. EOQ
    D. Both A and B

M O D U L E

III

Inventory Management Tools and Techniques

Learning Objectives

After completing this module, you will be able to

- List and describe tools and techniques of inventory management

- Understand the steps in calculating the standard deviation of the forecast error

- Write the formula for economic order quantity (EOQ)

FORECASTING AND DETERMINING INVENTORY LEVELS

In this module, various tools and techniques will be reviewed for determining the appropriate levels of inventory to buffer against fluctuations in demand and supply.

Forecasting is critical to estimating future demand. This estimate may be developed by using mathematical formulas, data from informal sources or a combination of both. Forecasting is key to all aspects of a successful business-planning system. As customers place more demands and require faster deliveries, the ability to forecast as accurately as possible is essential.

For forecasts to be usable, they must be based on timely data gathered in a consistent manner. A good forecasting process must include

- The use of forecasting tools e.g., using historical results to predict future sales

- The creation and collection of information

- The management of this information

- The making of well-informed decisions about what you need to produce

Forecasting is meaningful only if it helps to

- Improve customer service

- Reduce inventory

- Increase productivity

- Improve the deliveries from suppliers

Every good forecast includes an estimate of the forecast error. The forecast error is the difference between what you thought you were going to ship and what you actually shipped. In order to improve sales forecasts, you will first need to calculate the forecast error (actual sales minus forecasted sales equals forecast error). The larger the forecast error, the higher the level of inventory needed to satisfy customers.

FORECASTING AND DETERMINING INVENTORY LEVELS (continued)

Forecast Shipment Levels

Item	1 Actual	2 Forecast	3 Forecast Error	4 % Forecast Error
Product A	245	230	+15	+6.5%
Product F	110	120	−10	−8.3%
Total	355	350	+5	+1.4%

The entries below tell you what to do when you enter your own figures.

COLUMN	WHAT TO DO
1	Actual sales figures from the sales report.
2	Forecast figures from final forecast.
3	The forecast error is calculated for each period by subtracting column 2 from column 1.
4	The percentage of forecast error is calculated by dividing column 3 by column 2 (15 ÷ 230 = 6.5%).

In this example, the combined forecast error for Products A and F is equal to +1.4 percent. Marketing people would measure their success on the total forecast error of 1.4 percent, whereas manufacturing people would build products based on the individual product demand, and therefore would be affected by the forecast errors of each product. The forecast error can be averaged over the history of earlier periods to serve as the basis for determining what level of inventory you must carry to ensure a certain probability of shipping to a customer on time.

DETERMINING INVENTORY NEEDED

The more accurate your individual product sales forecasting is, the smaller your forecast error, and the less inventory you'll have to carry to maintain a specified level of customer service. By carrying less inventory, you can more effectively use the capacity of machines required to build the products. Inventory is not being built before needed, thus committing capacity of machines too early. By carrying less inventory, less space is used, and it is not used too early.

Since all forecasts have a forecast error, the next question is how to calculate the amount of inventory needed to buffer this forecast error and meet the company's objective of on-time shipment (i.e., customer service level).

▶ **Customer Service (Customer Service Ratio)** is a performance measure that is shown as a percentage of on-time versus promised delivery dates. It is stated both in dollars and units. Some companies call this the fill rate or order fill rate.

Another measure that is used in customer service is called the stockout rate or percentage. A stockout is the number of times each year that you run the risk of not having inventory when needed. The percentage of stockouts shows total stockout to total orders.

Customer service can also be looked at from the standpoint of "exposures" to stockouts. The number of stockouts can be calculated by dividing the annual usage by the lot size.

$$\text{Stockout} = \frac{\text{annual usage}}{\text{lot size}}$$

One of the most important tools used in determining the required inventory is the Standard Deviation of the Forecast Error calculation. The purpose of this calculation is to *calculate an amount of inventory that will allow for the forecast error and establish a certain probability of still shipping on time.*

▶ **Standard Deviation** is a statistical calculation that deals with difference. In the context of this book, it is the difference between forecasted shipments and actual shipments. This difference is called a forecast error. The standard deviation is shown in detail in Figure 3–1 on page 33.

DETERMINING INVENTORY NEEDED (continued)

► **Mean Absolute Deviation (MAD)** is a shorter version of the standard deviation calculation. To calculate MAD, simply total the forecast error, disregarding the fact that the forecast error is negative or positive. The sum of this total is then divided by the number of time periods being reviewed. The calculation of MAD is shown on page 34.

► **The Bias** shows a pattern of forecast errors (deviation) from the mean, either consistently too high or consistently too low. A good forecasting model should contain little or no bias.

► **Tracking Signal** is used to measure the "health" of your forecasting model. This measure is calculated by dividing the sum of the period forecast error by the mean absolute deviation.

This is not a recommended method for determining inventory needed!

The Role of Safety Stock

Safety stock is a quantity of stock to keep in inventory to protect against unexpected fluctuations in demand and/or supply. It is usually carried at the finished goods level. However, sometimes it is used to compensate for scrap and obsolete parts. Hard-to-get parts are carried as safety stock to guard against unreliable supplier deliveries. Safety lead time—which simply is an inflation of the lead time—is used sometimes to buffer against customer changes in the original lead time. Safety lead time and safety stock have the same effect on inventory; they both create demand for inventory before it is needed.

ESSENTIAL CALCULATIONS (STANDARD DEVIATION)

Review Figure 3–1, the History of Product A, which shows how to calculate the forecast error and the standard deviation of the forecast error.

	1	**2**	**3**	**4**
Time Periods*	**Actual Sales**	**Forecast**	**Forecast Error**	**Forecast Error^2 (squared)**
1	1520	1510	+10	100
2	1490	1500	−10	100
3	1510	1500	+10	100
4	1520	1500	+20	400
5	1470	1510	−40	1600
6	1510	1500	+10	100
			Total	2400

*Time period could be months or years.

Figure 3–1: History of Product A

Steps for Calculating Standard Deviation of the Forecast Error

STEP 1 To calculate forecast error, subtract column 2 from column 1.

STEP 2 Square each period's forecast error (column 3 × column 3). Remember, when you square a number, you multiply the number by itself.

STEP 3 Add all the entries/items in column 4. The total equals 2400.

STEP 4 Calculate the average of the square of the deviation (2400 ÷ 6 periods = 400).

STEP 5 Now find the square root sign ($\sqrt{}$) on your calculator, and determine the square root of 400.

ESSENTIAL CALCULATIONS (continued)

The Answer

The answer you should get is 20, which is the square root of 400. The answer, 20, is stated as one positive standard deviation. What this means is that if 20 units of inventory were held to buffer against the forecast error, a certain level of on-time shipments would have a probability of happening. Notice how small the inventory level is; this is because of the small forecast error.

The 20 units equal one positive standard deviation, and if this amount were to be carried in inventory, the probability of on-time shipments would be 84 out of 100 times, or 84% of the time.

For most customers, this would be totally unacceptable, and the supplier would be forced to carry at least two or three positive standard deviations, which would result in doubling or tripling the inventory investment—from 20 units to 40 units to 60 units. The result would be to increase the number of on-time shipments from 84% to 97.5% to 99.85% of the time (refer to Figure 3–2 on page 35).

Notice that as the inventory doubles and then triples, the on-time shipments increase at a diminishing rate.

Steps for Calculating Mean Absolute Deviation (MAD)

STEP 1 Add the forecast error in columns, disregarding the negative and positive signs (10 + 10 + 10 + 20 + 40 + 10 = 100).

STEP 2 Calculate the average of 100 (100 ÷ 6 periods = 16.7 rounded to 16).

STEP 3 Multiply 16 × 1.25 (the MAD factor for one positive deviation) = 20, which is equal to one standard deviation.

Inventory Level (units)	Standard Deviation	Mean Absolute Deviation	Customer Service Level
0	0.00	0.00	.50
20	1.00	1.25	.84
40	2.00	2.50	.975
60	3.00	3.75	.9985

Figure 3–2: Customer Service Level Table

And if you want to ship to customers 100% of the time (99.99967), the inventory would have to be increased six-fold (six positive deviations, aka 6 sigma) from 20 units to 120 units. Since going from three standard deviations to six will only increase your shipment levels by less than 1% but require doubling of the inventory from 60 to 120, companies may opt not to ship 100% of the time—just don't tell your customer!

THE 80/20 RULE (ABC ANALYSIS)

This law was discovered by Pareto, an Italian economist, approximately 500 years ago. He discovered that a small percentage of a population always has the greatest effect. Pareto's law was further expanded to the ABC classification that will be discussed in Module V and is summarized below. When considering how to apply this tool to establish inventory levels, consider the following: From a practical standpoint, ask yourself: "Which products (and which customers) generate 80 percent of the revenue?" *Answer: Approximately 20 percent of the products and customers generate 80 percent of the revenue.*

20% of customers, products, or parts =	80% of the company's revenue and inventory investment	These are called "A" customers "A" products "A" parts
30% of customers, products, or parts =	15% of the company's revenue and inventory investment	These are called "B"* customers "B" products "B" parts
50% of customers, products, or parts =	5% of the company's revenue and inventory investment	These are called "C"* customers "C" products "C" parts

*CAUTION—REMEMBER! *Don't* tell your customers they are B or C customers.

Note that the A customers still want the same level of shipments of your B and C products as they receive from the A products.

The fluctuation in demand for the B and C products causes most of the product mix problems, the changes on the shop floor (capacity) and the changes in the supplier due dates.

Consider doing the following:

☐ Reduce the forecast error by improving the forecast model.

☐ Use the standard deviation formula A customers and A and B parts.

☐ For C parts, give a predetermined number of days' supply and allow the production floor to build this during the beginning of each quarter.

The standard deviation of forecast error tool can also be used to determine

✓ The amount of extra (safety) lead time needed to ensure on-time delivery.

✓ The amount of work to release to the shop floor to make sure machines do not run out of work. That is, how much "queue" buffer is needed in back of the bottleneck work center.

✓ The number of extra (buffer) pieces to start on the initial machining operation to ensure a particular yield after the final operation (for example, scrap allowance).

✓ The amount of machine downtime (safety) to allow for in planning utilization of available capacity.

DETERMINING OTHER COSTS

There are additional costs associated with inventory, which include the cost to order, carry and store; stockout and transport inventory; as well as the costs of the inventory not being available when needed. Following is a summary of these costs and examples of each.

Ordering/Setup Cost

- Clerical work of preparing, issuing, following and receiving orders

- Physical handling of goods

- Inspection

- Machine setups (if manufactured)

Carrying Cost

- Obsolescence

- Deterioration

- Taxes (in some localities)

- Insurance

- Storage

- Capital

The cost of carrying inventory is usually defined as a percent of dollar value of inventory per unit of time (generally one year).

Storage Costs

- Utilities

- Warehouse/stockroom personnel

- Maintenance of building and equipment

- Warehouse security

Stockout Costs

- Expediting costs

- Freight premiums

- Back-order processing

- Difficult to determine because of intangible costs such as lost sales and customer goodwill

Transportation Costs

- Inventory tied up in transit

- Spoilage

- Damage

- Insurance

- Theft

- Handling

LOT SIZE AND SAFETY STOCK

Once the levels of inventory are determined, the next step is to calculate in what quantities the inventory will be replaced. This is called lot sizing. The lot size is the amount of material to be ordered from a supplier or produced internally to meet demand.

There are nine major types of lot-size methods, which fit into the following two categories:

► **Demand-based methods (static):** Order quantities are kept constant.

- Fixed order quantity: min/max

- Economic order quantity (EOQ): is calculated periodically and used as fixed order quantity during interim

► **Discrete method (dynamic):** Order quantities vary.

- Period order quantity

- Lot-for-lot

- Periods of supply

- Least unit cost

- Least total cost

- Part-period balancing

- Wagner-Whitin algorithm

Selecting the appropriate mix of lot-sizing methods will help to reduce ordering, setup and carrying costs, as well as reduce the overall levels of work-in-process inventory.

Each type of lot sizing methods will be reviewed using the information on page 41.

Lot Sizing Examples

All examples use the same set of forecast requirements:

- Starting inventory   = 800 units
- Order cost   = $20
- Item cost   = $2.50
- Annual carrying cost = 22%

Fixed Order Quantity

Fixed order quantity method will always suggest planned orders be released for a predetermined fixed quantity. The predetermined quantity can be established based on experience and/or the use of the economic order quantity technique. In the example below, the fixed order quantity is 300. (The actual MRP logic is explained in Module VI under MRP/DRP.) The reader, if unfamiliar with MRP logic, should read pages 97–101.

Fixed Order Quantity

Safety stock   =   40
Order quantity = 300
Lead time   =   2

		Periods					
		1	**2**	**3**	**4**	**5**	**6**
Forecast demand		380	320	300	200	230	320
Scheduled receipts							
Projected available	800	420	100	100	200	270	250
Net requirements				−200	−100	−30	−50
Planned order receipts				300	300	300	300
Planned order releases		300	300	300	300		

LOT SIZE AND SAFETY STOCK (continued)

Economic Order Quantity

The economic order quantity (EOQ) is the other type of demand-based or static formula. This calculation establishes the amount to be purchased or manufactured by determining the minimal cost of purchasing or building with the cost to carry the inventory.

The formula may be used to determine the minimum units to be purchased or built, or the minimum cost in dollars. Following are the two variations of this formula.

The EOQ Formula (Units and Dollars)

1. Units: $EOQ = \sqrt{\dfrac{2US}{IC}}$

where   U = Annual usage in units
S = Setup or ordering costs
I = Inventory carrying cost
C = Unit Cost

2. Dollars: $EOQ\$ = \sqrt{\dfrac{2AS}{I}}$

where   A = Annual usage in dollars
S = Setup or ordering cost
I = Inventory carrying cost

Economic Order Quantity

Annual usage = 3480
Order quantity = 500
Lead time = 2

		Periods					
		1	**2**	**3**	**4**	**5**	**6**
Forecast demand		380	320	300	200	220	320
Scheduled receipts							
Projected available	800	520	200	400	200	480	160
Net requirements				−100		−20	
Planned order receipts				500		500	
Planned order releases		500		500			

$A = 290 \times 12 = 3480$ $EOQ =$

$$\sqrt{\frac{2US}{CI}} = \sqrt{\frac{2 \times 3480 \times 20}{2.50 \times .22}} = \sqrt{253,091} = 503 \text{ (rounded to 500)}$$

The next six lot-sizing techniques are called discrete or dynamic lot-sizing techniques, because the lot sizes (quantity to be ordered) will vary.

LOT SIZE AND SAFETY STOCK (continued)

Period Order Quantity

Period order quantity is a lot-sizing technique in which the lot size is equal to the requirements for a given number of periods into the future. In the example below the number, of periods is determined to be 4.

Period Order Quantity

Order quantity = 630
Lead time = 2

		Periods					
		1	2	3	4	5	6
Forecast demand		130	160	120	260	130	120
Scheduled receipts							
Projected available	370	240	80	590	330	200	80
Net requirements				−40			
Planned order receipts				630			
Planned order releases		630					

$$POQ = \frac{EOQ}{\text{Average Period Usage}} = \frac{648}{162} = 4 = \text{Number of future periods covered}$$

The period order quantity is similar to the period of supply, except the order cycle is based on the EOQ calculation. The order frequency as well as the order quantities are scheduled using this method. The lot size of 630 covers four periods (period 3, 120 + period 4, 260 + period 5, 130 + period 6, 120 = 630).

Lot-for-Lot

This is an MRP lot-sizing technique commonly used in Just-in-Time (JIT) situations, in conjunction with safety stock. In this method, the planned orders are generated equal to the net requirements in each period. The safety stock level is determined by the standard deviation discussed earlier or is based on experience or trial and error.

Lot-for-Lot

Safety stock = 40
Order quantity = L4L
Lead time = 2

		Periods					
		1	2	3	4	5	6
Forecast demand		380	320	300	200	230	320
Scheduled receipts		380	320				
Projected available	40	40	40	40	40	40	40
Net requirements				−300	−200	−230	−320
Planned order receipts				300	200	230	320
Planned order releases		300	200	230	320		

Note that the lot-size quantity matches the amount required to meet the demand and cover the safety stock quantities.

LOT SIZE AND SAFETY STOCK (continued)

Periods of Supply

This method simply establishes—primarily through experience—an order quantity that will cover a predetermined period of time. In the example below it is for three periods.

Periods of Supply

		Periods				
		1	**2**	**3**	**4**	**5**
Forecast demand		380	320	300	200	220
Scheduled receipts						
Projected available	740	360	40	470	270	50
Net requirements				−300		
Planned order receipts				720		
Planned order releases		720				

Safety stock = 40
Order quantity = POS = 3
Lead time = 2

Note that the 730 will cover the demand for periods three, four, and five (300 + 200 + 220 = 720). The only difference between this method and period order quantity is that this method uses experience rather than the EOQ formula.

Least Unit Cost

The least unit cost method adds ordering cost and inventory-carrying cost for each trial lot size and divides by the number of units in the lot size. The lot size with the lowest unit cost is chosen.

Least Total Cost

The least total cost lot-sizing technique calculates the order quantity by comparing the set (or ordering) costs and the carrying costs for various lot sizes, and selects the lot size where these costs are most nearly equal.

Part-Period Balancing

This technique is similar to the least total cost method. However, this method employs a routine called look ahead/look back. When the look ahead/look back feature is used, a lot quantity is calculated, and before it is firmed up, the next or previous period is reviewed to determine whether it would be economical to include either in the current lot.

Wagner-Whitin Algorithm

The final method is the Wagner-Whitin algorithm. This is a very complex method that evaluates all possible ways to cover the requirements in each period of the planning horizon.

EXERCISE 1: Calculations

Complete the following calculations. See pages 112–113 in the back of the book for the correct answers.

1. Determine the following order quantities, based on dollars and units.

EOQ Example

U = Annual usage in units = 5,500

A = Annual usage in dollars = $60,000

S = Setup cost/ordering cost = $100

I = Inventory carrying cost = $0.20

C = Unit cost = $10

A. Dollars

Dollars: $EOQ\$ = \sqrt{\dfrac{2AS}{I}}$

where: A = Annual usage
in dollars
B = Setup or
ordering cost
I = Inventory
carrying cost

B. Units

Units: $EOQ = \sqrt{\dfrac{2US}{IC}}$

where: U = Annual usage
in units
S = Setup or
ordering cost
I = Inventory
carrying cost
C = Unit Cost

2. Calculate the standard deviation of the forecast error and mean absolute deviation (MAD). Complete the tables below with your calculations.

Time Period	Forecast	Sales	Forecast Error	Forecast Error^2
1	500	600		
2	500	500		
3	500	400		
4	500	450		
5	500	700		
6	500	600		
7	500	550		
8	500	500		
9	500	350		
10	500	450		
Total	5,000	5,100		

A. Calculate the standard deviation forecast error.

B. Calculate the mean absolute deviation (MAD).

EXERCISE 2: Fill In the Blanks

Part A: *Using the Customer Service Level Table below, plot the amount of inventory that will be needed to provide various levels of on-time shipments. Complete the chart below, which reinforces this concept. See page 113 in the back of the book for the correct answer.*

Standard Deviation	Mean Absolute Deviation	Customer Service Level
0.00	0.00	.50
1.00	1.25	.84
2.00	2.50	.975
3.00	3.75	.9985

Customer Service Level Table

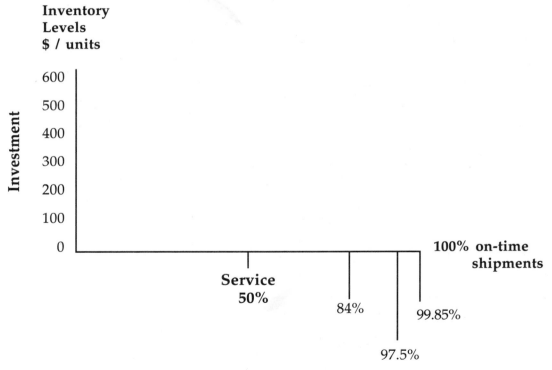

Part B: How much inventory would be needed to cover six standard deviations, which would give a customer service level of as close to 100 percent as possible? _____

Remember, these inventory levels represent one positive deviation.

If you don't like the answer, try improving your forecast model.

EXERCISE 3: *Choose the Correct Answer*

Answer the following questions. See page 113 in the back of the book for the correct answers.

1. MAD is

    A. Mean absolute deviation
    B. Not as precise as the standard deviation
    C. Easier to calculate than standard deviation
    D. All of the above

2. Using the following customer service level table, and assuming the standard deviation was 200 and MAD was 160, determine the inventory level of three positive deviations.

Inventory Level (units)	Standard Deviation	Mean Absolute Deviation	Customer Service Level
0	0.00	0.00	.50
200	1.00	1.25	.84
400	2.00	2.50	.975
600	3.00	3.75	.9985

    A. 3 positive standard deviations equal 600
    B. An inventory level of 200 equal a MAD factor of 1.25
    C. One positive standard deviation equals 1.25 MAD
    D. All of the above

3. All of the following are types of lot-sizing techniques *except*

    A. Least unit cost
    B. Least cost
    C. Part period balancing
    D. EOQ

EXERCISE 3 (continued)

4. Which of the following are included in storage costs?

    A. Utilities
    B. Warehouse/stockroom personnel
    C. Warehouse security
    D. All of the above

5. All of the following are included in stockout costs *except*

    A. Expediting cost
    B. Back orders
    C. Interest expense
    D. Freight premiums

M O D U L E

IV

Inventory Management and Financial Analysis

Learning Objectives

After completing this module, you will be able to

- Describe major inventory classifications

- Complete an analysis of a balance sheet and income statement

- Write the formula for the basic manufacturing equation and describe how inventory impacts it

FINANCIAL CONTROL OF INVENTORY

One of the areas frequently overlooked in the preparation of manufacturing professionals is their financial knowledge. Experience has shown it is not necessary to master a level of detail such as the accounting rules of debits and credits. However, at a minimum it is necessary to understand the financial ramifications of financial discussions and decisions. By becoming familiar with financial statements, you begin to develop "a feel" for the information.

The following should be understood:

► Financial Statements: Types and components of Balance Sheet and Income Statement

► Key Ratios and Formulas Such as Inventory Turns: How to improve them and their impact on cash flow

► Basic Manufacturing Equation:
  Beginning Inventory
  + Production (transfers in)
  = Available to ship (use)
  – Shipments (transfers out)
  = Ending Inventory

► Costed Bill of Materials

► Activity-Based Costing

MAPSON

BALANCE SHEET BASICS

The Balance Sheet is a statement—as of a specific date, for example, December 31—of what the company owns (assets), what it owes in debts (liabilities) and the difference between these two (assets minus liabilities), which is called the stockholder equity (net worth).

Balance Sheet Components

Assets—Items the company owns. Assets are divided into short-term (consumed in less than a year) and long-term (have value for more than one year). Examples of short-term assets are cash, accounts receivable and inventory. Examples of long-term assets are machines and equipment.

Liabilities—These are debts owed. Liabilities are divided into short-term and long-term. Short-term liabilities includes accounts payable and taxes payable. Payment is due monthly. Long-term liabilities include the acquisition of buildings. Payment is spread out over years.

Shareholders' Equity—Contains the value of the ownership of the stockholders (owners) and the earnings and losses the company has incurred since the company was started (retained earnings).

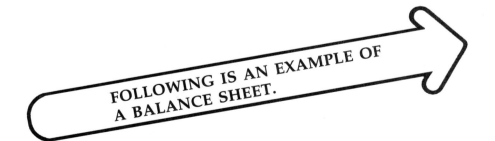

FOLLOWING IS AN EXAMPLE OF A BALANCE SHEET.

Sample Balance Sheet
(In millions of dollars)

	Prior year	Current		Prior year	Current
Current Assets (000)			**Current Liabilities**		
Cash	80	100	Accounts Payable	100	300
Accts receivable	160	200	Short-term debt	120	400
Inventories			**Total current liabilities**	220	700
Raw materials	60	100			
Work-in-process	60	400	**Long-term Liabilities**		
Finished goods	90	215	Long-term debt	315	440
Total inventories	210	715	**TOTAL LIABILITIES**	535	1,140
Total Current Assets	450	1,015			
			Shareholders' Equity		
Property, Plant and Equipt.			Common stock	53	55
Land	45	50	Accumulated retained		
Buildings	220	340	earnings	487	565
Machinery, equipt., tools	535	610			
Total Prop., Plant Equipt.	800	1,000	**Total Shareholders' Equity**	540	620
Less accum depreciation	(175)	(255)			
Net Property, Plant, Equipt.	625	745			
			Total Liabilities and		
TOTAL ASSETS	1,075	1,760	**Shareholders' Equity**	1,075	1,760

USEFUL TIPS FOR READING A BALANCE SHEET

► The Balance Sheet is a statement—as of a specific date, for example, December 31, 19XX—of what the company owns (assets), what it owes in debts (liabilities) and the difference between these two (assets minus liabilities), which is called the stockholders' equity (net worth).

► The assets are always listed in order of liquidity—how fast they could be turned into cash.

► The assets are divided into short-term assets (cash, accounts receivable, inventory, and so on) and long-term assets (machinery and equipment [less depreciation], facilities, land and so on).

► The liabilities are always listed in the order in which the creditors would have claims against the assets should bankruptcy occur.

► Liabilities are broken into short-term liabilities—accounts payable, accrued payroll, short-term notes and so on; and long-term liabilities—long-term debt and so on.

► The total of the stockholders' equity section of the Balance Sheet must always represent the total assets minus total liabilities; so the following equation is always in balance:

Assets – Liabilities = Stockholders' Equity, more commonly shown as the basic accounting equation: Assets = Liabilities + Stockholders' Equity

► The stockholders' equity components are always listed in the order in which the stockholders would be paid after the creditors, if the corporation were liquidated. For example, preferred stockholders would be paid before common stockholders.

► The retained earnings section of the stockholders' equity balance sheet represents the accumulation of all the profits and losses since the corporation's inception.

INCOME STATEMENT BASICS

The second type of financial statement is the Income Statement. This statement shows revenue (how much the company has earned year to date), Cost of Sales (how much it cost to produce the products sold), Gross Profit (determined by subtracting the Cost of Sales from the Revenue). All other expenses are included in the Sales, General and Administrative Expenses (commonly referred to as SG&A) The net profit is determined by subtracting the SG&A expense for the Gross Profit. Following is an example of an Income Statement.

Sample Income Statement (In millions of dollars)	Prior year	Current year
Sales	$2,000	$1,600
Cost of Sales and Operating Expenses		
Cost of goods sold	1,300	900
Gross profit	700	700
Selling, general, and administrative expenses	320	240
Operating profit	380	460
Other Income (expenses)		
Interest expense	−60	−20
Provision for Federal Income Taxes	−140	−200
Net Income	180	240

USEFUL TIPS FOR READING AN INCOME STATEMENT

► The Income Statement is a statement of revenue less expenses, with the difference between the two (hopefully) being a profit (revenues greater than expenses).

► Revenues result from the sales of items scheduled to be shipped in the Master Production Schedule.

► If discounts or allowances for quantity sales are granted, these amounts would be subtracted from the revenue line, and the result would be net sales.

► The expenses are divided into the major categories of Cost of Sales, then Sales, General, and Administrative Expenses.

► The Cost of Sales includes the cost of the goods manufactured, which is made up of: Direct Material, Direct labor, and Factory Overhead.

► The difference between Net Revenue and Cost of Goods Sold is called Gross Profit. The Sales, General and Administrative Expense (SG&A) include all other expenses not included in Cost of Sales.

► The expenses for selling the product, general administrative expenses, and all other expenses are subtracted from the gross profit to give the profit before taxes or the loss the company incurred for the current one-year period.

► The profit remaining after taxes, or the loss, is then transferred to retained earnings in the Balance Sheet when the books are closed for the year.

EXERCISE 1: *Observations*

Refer back to the Sample Balance Sheet on page 57. List three observations regarding the Balance Sheet. The first one has been done for you.

- Assets are listed in order of liquidity _____

- _____

- _____

- _____

Now list three changes from one year to the next.

- Total assets have more than doubled from previous year to the current.

- _____

- _____

- _____

If you have trouble with this, reread "Useful Tips for Reading a Balance Sheet."

62

THE BASIC MANUFACTURING EQUATION

The basic manufacturing equation, which is nothing more than an accounting formula with units replacing dollars, says: Beginning inventory, plus what is planned to be built for the period, equals what is available to be sold. From the amount available to sell, customer orders as well as marketing forecasts are subtracted to arrive at the ending inventory. The inventory level in this formula would vary, depending on whether the product or service being sold was built-to-stock (there would be Finished Goods) or built-to-customer-order (there should be little or no inventory). From an accounting standpoint, this formula must be in balance at the end of each month and at year end, in order to close the books.

This basic manufacturing formula requires three sets of figures: projected sales, beginning and ending inventory levels, and production levels. Following is an example of the manufacturing formula.

Step	Basic Manufacturing Formula	Units	Dollars* (millions)
4	Beginning inventory	1,000	$ 1,000
5	+ Production levels (build plan)	9,500	9,500
3	= Available inventory to ship (at cost)	10,500	10,500
1	– Shipments/Sales (cost of sales)	10,000	10,000
2	= Ending inventory	500	500

*The assumption is a unit cost of $1,000

The steps for determining the numbers in the basic manufacturing formula are as follows:

STEP 1   First you need to establish projected shipments/sales for the year. Your top executives establish the sales required to meet the business objectives for growth, market share and so on. In this example, the projected shipment is 10,000 units (at cost).

STEP 2   Next, you must set ending inventory levels. Inventory levels are based on two requirements:

- The desired level of customer satisfaction, i.e., how many times can you ship when the customer wants the product shipped. This topic will be discussed in detail in the Module III.

- Forecast error (discussed in Module III), which refers to the difference between forecasted sales and actual sales (fluctuation in demand).

In this example, the projected (forecasted) ending inventory level is 500 units.

STEP 3   When you have determined the desired level of shipments and have projected the ending inventory levels, you can determine the available inventory units to ship by adding the shipment of 10,000 units to the projected ending inventory level of 500 units. The available inventory to ship is equal to 10,500 units.

STEP 4   The beginning inventory for the year is taken directly from the ending inventory of the previous year. In this example, it is a given, 1,000 units.

STEP 5   You can now determine the production for the year by subtracting the beginning inventory (1,000 units) from the available-to-ship inventory (10,500 units). In this example, the production is 9,500 units.

KEY FINANCIAL RATIOS

The following charts show the major calculations of key financial ratios: liquidity, leverage and profitability. Within each of these categories are examples of the ratios, methods of calculations and a short list of industry standards and their significance.

Key Financial Ratios

Name	Method of Calculation	Standard & Significance
LIQUIDITY		
Current Ratio	$\dfrac{\text{Current Assets}}{\text{Current Liabilities}}$	Industry average: Low—possible cash flow problems; High–may not be managing assets well.
Quick Ratio	$\dfrac{\text{Cash + Receivables}}{\text{Current Liabilities}}$	Low—cash flow problems; High—may mean poor asset management.
Days Sales Outstanding (DSO)	$\dfrac{\text{Receivables} \times 365}{\text{Net Sales}}$	High hurts cash flow; Very low—too restrictive credit policies.
Inventory Turnover	$\dfrac{\text{Cost of Sales}}{\text{Inventory}}$	Industry average: Low—problems with slow inventory which may hurt cash flow; Very high—may run out of inventory.
LEVERAGE		
Debt-to-Equity	$\dfrac{\text{Total Liabilites}}{\text{Equity}}$	Industry average
PROFITABILITY		
Return on Equity	$\dfrac{\text{Net Income}}{\text{Equity}}$	The higher the better: The return on the shareholders' investment in the business.
Return on Assets	$\dfrac{\text{Net Income}}{\text{Total Assets}}$	Industry average: Return the company earns on everything it owns.

EXERCISE 2: *Calculating Ratios*

A. Using the Financial Statements on pages 57 and 59, calculate the following ratios. (Round all numbers to the nearest 100th.) See page 114 in the back of the book for the correct answers.

Key Financial Ratios

NAME	METHOD OF CALCULATION	ANSWERS Prior Year	Current Year
Liquidity Current Ratio	$\dfrac{\text{Current Assets}}{\text{Current Liabilities}}$		
Quick Ratio	$\dfrac{\text{Cash + Receivables}}{\text{Current Liabilities}}$		
Days Sales Outstanding (DSO)	$\dfrac{\text{Receivables} \times 365}{\text{Net Sales}}$		
Inventory Turnover	$\dfrac{\text{Cost of Goods Sold}}{\text{Inventory}}$		
Leverage Debt-to-Equity	$\dfrac{\text{Total Liabilites}}{\text{Equity}}$		
Profitability Return on Equity	$\dfrac{\text{Net Income}}{\text{Equity}}$		
Return on Assets	$\dfrac{\text{Net Income}}{\text{Total Assets}}$		

B. List five questions you might ask based on your observations of the Balance Sheet from the prior exercise.

1. _____

2. _____

3. _____

4. _____

5. _____

FINANCIAL EVALUATION CHECKLIST

Following are questions one might ask when evaluating financial statements.

Balance Sheet

☐ **Inventory**—How is it valued (LIFO, FIFO, standard)? Likelihood of obsolescence?

☐ **Accounts Receivable**—What is its aging? Is there a particular customer that makes up that aging? (Methods of inventory valuations are covered later in this module.)

☐ **Fixed Assets**—Method of depreciation, useful lives used, how heavily depreciated?

☐ **Accounts Payable**—Who are major suppliers? Terms and quality of the relationship? How quickly are bills paid?

☐ **Short-Term Debt**—How much? What are the terms and conditions?

☐ **Long-Term Debt**— Interest rate, repayment requirements; is the part due in the next year shown as a current liability?

☐ **Other Liabilities**—Are adequate reserves established for warranties, environmental costs, litigation in progress?

☐ **Equity**—Who are major shareholders? Likelihood of change in ownership or takeover?

Income Statement

☐ Read the profit and loss statement. What is Cost of Sales (COS) as a % of sales (COS = direct materials/direct labor/factory overhead). What is gross profit as a % of sales (sales – COS)? What is SG&A as a % of sales?

☐ Evaluate major cost items as a % of sales and compare to industry data. Are expenses reasonable and in proportion?

☐ What operating lease commitments (i.e., leases not shown on balance sheet) are there?

☐ What portion of the depreciation expense is the company charged relative to its use of the fixed assets?

Other Issues

☐ Major litigation?

☐ Any other significant events?

IDENTIFYING SUPPLIERS WITH POTENTIAL CASH-FLOW PROBLEMS

To ensure on-time delivery to your customers, you need to be confident that your supplier is financially healthy enough to get your orders filled. Answers to the following questions can help you identify suppliers with a potential cash-flow problem.

- Is a start-up or rapidly growing company.

- Has slow-paying customers or heavy dependence on one slow-paying customer. (Check the DSO [day's sales outstanding] ratio.)

- Has high levels of inventory.

- Is rapidly expanding to meet customer demands.

- Has a heavy investment requirement in new technology.

- Has insufficient knowledge of its costs and, as a result, inappropriate pricing.

- Has poor internal cost controls.

Following are some symptoms of a company's cash-flow problems:

- Has a series of slow payments or CODs on a Dun & Bradstreet report.

- Stops taking advantage of discounts for early payment.

- Has problems making delivery schedules.

- Factors its receivables (i.e., sells them to a bank or finance company).

- Requests early payment from customers.

- Has inventory that appears to be moving slowly. (Check the inventory turnover ratio and, if possible, the inventory aging.)

- Has low current and acid-test ratios.

- Has difficulties meeting commitments to its lenders. (Check the debt-to-equity and debt-service ratios. Also check the banking statement on the D & B to see if the bank indicates any problems.)

COSTED BILL OF MATERIALS

The following example shows a costed bill of materials (BOM). From this, a cost buildup can be completed.

Costed Bill of Materials (BOM)

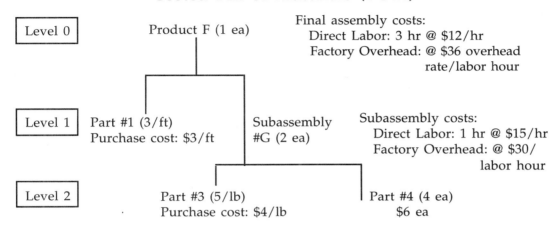

| Level 0 | Product F (1 ea) | Final assembly costs:
Direct Labor: 3 hr @ $12/hr
Factory Overhead: @ $36 overhead
rate/labor hour |

| Level 1 | Part #1 (3/ft)
Purchase cost: $3/ft | Subassembly #G (2 ea) | Subassembly costs:
Direct Labor: 1 hr @ $15/hr
Factory Overhead: @ $30/
labor hour |

| Level 2 | Part #3 (5/lb)
Purchase cost: $4/lb | Part #4 (4 ea)
$6 ea |

Cost Roll-up (bottom up)

Part #	Material $	Labor $	Over-head $	Total $
Subassembly G:				
From Part #3: 5 lb × $4/lb	20			20
From Part #4: 4 ea × $6 ea	24			24
Labor: 1 hr × $15/hr		15		15
Overhead: 1 hr × #30/hr			30	30
Subtotal of G	**44**	**15**	**30**	**89**
Final Assembly F costs:				
From Part #1: 3 ft × $3/ft	9			9
From Subassembly G:	44	15	30	89
Labor to assembly F: 3 hr × $12/hr		36		36
Overhead to assemble F: 3 hr × $36/hr			108	108
Total end item F costs	**53**	**51**	**138**	**242**

COSTED BILL OF MATERIALS (continued)

Explanation of Cost Buildup Product F (1 unit)

Starting at level 2, there are purchased parts #3 and #4, with a purchased cost of $4 and $6, respectively.

When parts #3 and #4 are delivered to a work center, Direct Labor is charged at a stated cost of 1 hour at $15 per hour. Factory Overhead is added at a standard cost of $30 per labor hour. The total cost of Subassembly G is $89 ($20 for part #3, $24 for part #4, $15 for Direct Labor, and $30 for Factory Overhead).

The cost buildup continues by combining part #1 with subassembly G, which would result in product F and a total cost of $242 ($89 for subassembly G, $9 material costs for part #1, and $36 direct labor × 3 hours equals $108 of factory overhead).

In summary, Direct Labor is the labor costs involved by those actually putting the product together; Factory Overhead includes all the other costs—salaries of purchasing, information services people, managers, depreciation and other.

Questions to Ask When Reviewing a Costed Bill of Materials

☐ What is the percentage of material cost in the BOM?

☐ How do you make the overhead allocation?

☐ As the learning curve improves, does the allocation change?

☐ Can costly processes be subcontracted; what are they?

☐ What is the queue time between steps in the routing (assembly of this end item)?

☐ Are there common parts in this process? (If so, how many and at what levels are they located?)

☐ What value analysis is being performed to reduce the cost?

☐ What is the budgeted labor productivity improvement?

☐ What is the cost driver for each assembly area? (Assuming Activity-Based Costing is being used)

☐ What is the capacity at each work center?

☐ What is the bottleneck work center?

☐ What are the plans for reducing costs at each level?

☐ Are the processes standardized?

☐ Do custom requirements cost your company or your suppliers more to process?

☐ What is the premium to pay as a result?

☐ How many inspections are in the process?

☐ How often do you revise the standard costs?

☐ How many rework steps or operations are there at subcontractors or within the company's operation?

☐ What is the information flow?

☐ What is the physical process flow?

☐ What pieces of equipment are used for my product?

ALLOCATION OF FACTORY OVERHEAD AND ACTIVITY-BASED COSTING

In many companies, the total of factory overhead is growing faster than the other major Cost of Sales (COS) items—i.e., Direct Labor and Direct Material. In the past, these overhead costs had been allocated to products or product lines based on direct labor or machine run-time per unit, subassembly, assembly, etc. But because of significant reduction in direct labor content and changes in machine technology, a new method of allocating overhead was required. This method was called *activity-based costing*. When coupled with the concept of cost drivers, a more equitable way of allocating overhead costs resulted. Examples of cost drivers are head count, complexity of the preparation of the purchase order, line items on a P.O., etc.

The result of using activity-based costing does not change the overall profit or loss of a company, but it does more fairly allocate a major component of cost of sales—overhead—thus presenting a more precise statement of product line profitability as opposed to the company's overall profitability.

Inventory Valuation

The actual value of inventory using generally accepted accounting principles is computed using one of three basic approaches: first-in-first-out (FIFO), last-in-first-out (LIFO), or a standard cost system. In project or government orders, actual costs are charged directly to work being performed (work orders). This method is sometimes called "order specific costing" and is usually used when large, expensive items or projects are involved.

Some companies inadvertently use an inventory system called "FISH"—first-in-still-here. This is not recommended by the author!

Note that the above accounting methods are used only to value the inventory on the Balance Sheet and the Income Statement, not to determine the sequence in which material is used.

FIFO assumes inventory leaves in the same order as it arrives; oldest goods leave first. LIFO assumes the most recent arrivals in inventory are consumed first. In other words, the last items into inventory are the first to be charged to the COS.

In FIFO, inventory on the balance sheet is based on the newest parts to come in; in LIFO it is the oldest item.

Valuing inventory at standard cost involves recording the inventory or the Balance Sheet and COS at a predetermined rate for material, direct labor and overhead. These predetermined rates are called "standards." If significant "variances" occur between actual prices, the inventory and COS are adjusted up or down. This is usually done by the accounting department on a monthly or quarterly basis.

Two other systems that are used occasionally are the replacement cost system and the average cost system.

The replacement cost system projects an inventory cost based on a projected cost to replace items.

The average or weighted average cost system assigns the value to inventory based on the total number of each inventory item purchased at a specific cost.

Inventory is valued at either its original cost or its current market value, whichever is lower. This conservative accounting approach gives recognition to the fact that inventory values can change with time and can decrease in value because of such factors as time, obsolescence, etc.

EXERCISE 3: *Valuing Inventory*

In the following exercise, on a separate piece of paper, determine the value of the inventory. See page 115 in the back of the book for the correct answers.

Purchases

Month	Quantity	Unit Cost
January	1000	$4.00
February	2000	4.20
March	1000	4.20
April	1500	4.40
May	1000	4.50
June	2000	4.50
Total	**8500**	

Beginning on-hand inventory = 0
4000 units were sold during the first half of the year.
Standard cost: $4.40
Expected replacement value per unit is $4.65.

Determine the value of the 4000 units using LIFO, FIFO, standard cost, and replacement values in the space below.

EXERCISE 4: *Choose the Correct Answer*

Complete the following exercise. See page 116 in the back of the book for the correct answers.

1. Inventory carrying costs include which of the following items?

   I. Cost of capital
   II. Taxes and insurance
   III. Obsolescence

   A. I and II
   B. II and III
   C. All of the above

2. An inventory valuation method that uses standard cost is

   I. LIFO
   II. FISH
   III. FIFO

   A. I and II
   B. All of the above
   C. None of the above

3. Which of the following properly states the basic accounting equation?

   A. Assets = Liabilities + Stockholders' Equity
   B. Beginning Inventory + Production – Shipments = Ending Inventory
   C. EOQ

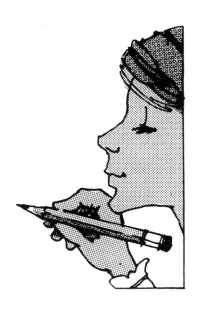

MODULE
V

Physical Controls: The Warehouse Environment

Learning Objectives

After completing this module, you will be able to

- Explain the objectives of warehousing
- Describe the types of warehousing
- Define major warehousing activites

OBJECTIVES OF WAREHOUSING

Warehousing is intended to maximize customer service by positioning the inventory as close to the customer as possible while still impacting cost reductions, especially in the transportation area. Additional objectives include the efficiency of the warehouse operation, maximizing the utilization of warehouse space, and maximizing profit. In addition to the physical control and security of the parts and products, good space utilization is another major objective.

Types of Warehouses

The two major types of warehouses are those located at or near the manufacturing facilities and those located in the "field." Field warehouses are geographically located to serve customers through quicker access and product delivery capabilities. They can provide a significant competitive advantage.

Field warehouses include those run by suppliers, wholesalers, and retailers and those classified as public warehouses. Field warehouses may be further broken down geographically by region, area and district.

Warehouses may be intended to simply store goods for long periods of time, or they may be used to improve the distribution of products. In addition to facilitating the movement of goods, field warehouses may be used to unpack and repack goods. Reducing lead time through field warehouses is a major objective.

WAREHOUSE LAYOUT FOR OPTIMAL EFFICIENCY

When designing a warehouse, the following items need to be considered in order to ensure optimal utilization and efficiency:

- Space for storing the items

- Areas for receiving, and shipping docks

- Areas for staging, picking, assembly and packaging

- Equipment

The physical structure and the warehouse layout are a compromise of storage and handling efficiencies. If inventory turns are low, with a lot of slow-moving items, the storage is important. If, on the other hand, inventory turns are high, with a lot of fast-moving items, then handling efficiency is important.

Another way of optimizing efficiencies is to schedule deliveries in a staggered approach throughout the day.

Finally, equipment such as forklift trucks and order-picking systems are assets that must be properly utilized, by proper scheduling.

Establishing a System for Locating Parts (Locator System)

After the warehouse layout is established, a system for locating parts is established by creating a system that identifies the location of each item in the warehouse.

Once a system for the overall location of parts has been established, it must be further refined by choosing one of two basic ways of assigning locations for items being stored. The first method is called fixed location; the second is the floating location system.

Fixed Location Systems

SKUs (stockkeeping units) are assigned permanent locations. No other goods are stored there. This method does not meet the full utilization objective, but it does make it easy to remember in what general area items are located. As a result, products can be located and retrieved faster. This system also requires less information processing. This system is most practical in situations where space is not an issue.

Floating Location Systems

The product is stored in a random fashion, based on space availability. In this system the same SKUs can be stored in several locations. This type of system relies on computer systems to keep track of the physical locations of items. The cost of the computer system is offset by better space utilization and faster access retrieval.

Physical Control (Cycle Counting) and Information Systems

Once a part or product is received and stored, it must be controlled both physically and financially. Physical inventory control is accomplished by restricting access to the inventory and counting what is physically on hand. Physical inventories can be taken on a continuous or periodic basis. Most companies today control inventory by updating the physical activity so that the status of the physical inventory on hand can be reconciled to the accounting records at any time. This reconciliation with accounting records results in financial control over inventory, as well as physical control.

Because of legal requirements, all companies take a partial or a complete physical inventory at least once a year.

WAREHOUSE LAYOUT FOR OPTIMAL EFFICIENCY (continued)

Cycle Counting

Cycle counting is a common way of controlling physical inventory. Most effective cycle-counting systems require the counting of a certain number of items every workday, with each item counted at a prescribed frequency.

Most cycle-counting systems determine the frequency of counting parts based on the value of usage. An ABC classification system is used. This system groups items in decreasing order of annual dollar volume (unit price × projected volume). Items are normally split into three categories, called A, B, and C. (This process is also called a Pareto Analysis.)

"A" items have the highest value. These are relatively few items (15–20 percent) whose value accounts for 75–80 percent of the total value of the inventory. As a general rule, 20 percent of the items constitute 80 percent of the annual requirements. All "A" items are counted monthly.

"B" items have medium value. These are a larger number in the middle of the list, usually about 30-40 percent of the items, accounting for about 15 percent of the value. All "B" items are counted quarterly.

"C" items have low value. These are the bulk of the inventory, usually about 40–50 percent of the items, whose total inventory value is almost negligible, accounting for only 5–10 percent of the value. All "C" items are counted annually. Many times these physical counts are based on estimates.

ABC Analysis Calculation Steps

1. Calculate annual usage in units for each item.

2. Multiply usage by unit cost to determine annual dollar usage.

3. Rank annual dollar usage from highest to lowest.

4. Assign ABC categories.

EXERCISE 1: Fill In the Charts

1. *In this exercise you will use an ABC classification analysis. First, multiply column 1 by column 2 to determine the annual usage in dollars. See pages 116–117 in the back of the book for the correct answers.*

ABC Analysis Based on Annual Dollar Volume
Annual Dollar Volume Percentages

	1	2	3	4
Item	Unit Cost	Annual Usage (units)	Annual Usage (dollars)	% of Total Dollar Usage
1	$4.00	1,250		
2	2.50	1,500		
3	3.00	10,000		
4	36.00	4,000		
5	31.00	12,500		
6	.517	8,000		
7	25.00	1,480		
8	325.00	100		
9	8.00	625		
10	6.00	1,000		
		Total		100%

2. *Now rank the answers from the highest annual dollar usage to the lowest.*

	1	2	3	4
Item	Annual Usage (dollars)	% of Total	Cumulative %	Classification

PICKING, PACKING, AND SHIPPING

When parts or products are ready to be pulled (picked) from inventory and sent out of the warehouse, several methods can be used.

▶ One method is to set up zones (areas) in the warehouse and assign one person to each area. Each person is responsible for picking in their designated floor-space area. Depending on the volume and security issues, these same individuals may be responsible for also storing incoming items.

▶ A modification to this method is called a sequential zone system. The order to be placed is broken down by zones and then pulled in sequence, one zone after the next.

▶ Random picking is used in smaller warehouses. The order picker moves through the warehouse pulling items from the list (pick list) of items to be pulled.

▶ When parts and products are pulled for use, they may require repackaging. This is done to prevent damage, especially if they are being sent over long distances.

▶ A final level of packing is the consolidation of all the packages into what is called a unit load. Pallets and ocean-going containers are examples of unit loads.

▶ The added cost of this packaging and repackaging process must be compared to the increased efficiency in handling and transporting the package.

▶ The greater the number of units that fit into a storage space, the greater the utilization and the less the unit cost.

COSTS OF WAREHOUSING

Warehousing costs are commonly broken down into two major categories: processing costs and storage costs (space).

Processing costs include the cost of receiving, storing, picking, packaging and shipping. If any type of assembly is performed in the warehouse, this cost must also be included.

Storage costs will be looked at in more detail in Module VI, when the additional cost of transportation and inventory-carrying costs are considered in a total system cost discussion.

Location of Warehouses and Distribution Centers

Regional and area distribution centers (field warehouses) are located based on competitive requirements, such as faster delivery and lower transportation costs.

When determining the number and the size of the distribution centers, costs for land, buildings and transportation must be calculated.

The following formula provides a rough calculation of the safety stock necessary, relative to the number of distribution centers at any one level in the distribution system, and shows that there is an inverse relationship between the numbers of distribution centers and the size of those distribution centers.

$$\text{Safety Stock (for EACH Distribution Center)} = \frac{\text{Safety Stock for ONE Distribution Center}}{\sqrt{\text{Number of Distribution Centers}}}$$

For example, if a company were carrying 200 units of safety stock at one distribution center and decided to add 15 additional distribution centers, the required safety stock for each distribution center would be

$$\text{Safety Stock} = \frac{200}{\sqrt{16}} = \frac{200}{4} = 50$$

Accordingly, the total amount of safety stock for the company would equal

$$\text{Total Safety Stock} = 50 \times 16 = 800$$

COSTS OF WAREHOUSING (continued)

Qualitative and Quantitative Costs

Many factors come into play when locating a warehouse. Two major categories are those considered qualitative factors and those considered quantitative factors.

Quantitative costs are costs which can be calculated, such as the costs to build facilities.

Qualitative costs are costs based on estimates of perceived value. Many times these costs are assigned numerically weighted values rather than dollar values. An example of a qualitative cost would be the proximity of universities and colleges.

CASE STUDY, PART 1: JADE Inc.

JADE Inc. has hired you. Your assignment is to present a list of quantitative factors and qualitative factors that should be considered in making the decision about where to locate their new warehouse.

---

1. List five examples of quantitative costs:

   - _____
   - _____
   - _____
   - _____
   - _____

2. List five examples of qualitative costs:

   - _____
   - _____
   - _____
   - _____
   - _____

See page 117 in the back of the book for suggested responses.

SETTING UP A WAREHOUSE SYSTEM

When setting up a warehouse system, one of the first issues to be considered is how to locate parts and products as they are received into the warehouse.

First divide the items into slow- and fast-moving parts. The fast-moving items should be located close to the receiving and shipping docks. The slow-moving parts and products should be located in areas where ease of access is not as important.

In addition to dividing parts and products into fast- and slow-moving items, consider the size and similarity of items: small packages on shelves, bulk items in designated bulk areas, and speciality items such as gases stored according to government specifications.

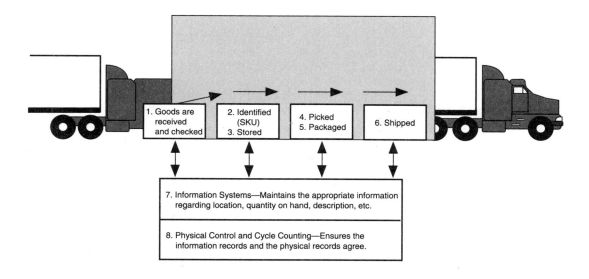

Figure 5.1 Inventory movement through a warehouse

EXERCISE 2: *Choose the Correct Answer*

Answer the following questions. See page 118 in the back of the book for the correct answers.

1. Which of the following best describes cycle counting?

    I. Inventory audit technique
    II. Used instead of a perpetual inventory
    III. Uses ABC analysis for determining items to be counted
    IV. The purpose is to find and correct errors

    A. I only
    B. I, II and III
    C. I, III and IV

2. List the major warehouse activities:

_____

_____

_____

3. What are the two types of systems for locating parts?

_____

_____

4. Which of the following areas are considered major types of warehouse processing costs?

    I. Receiving
    II. Picking
    III. Packaging
    IV. Shipping

    A. I only
    B. I and II
    C. II, III and IV
    D. All of the above

CASE STUDY, PART 2: JADE Inc.

JADE Inc. was so impressed with your first job they asked you back to recommend a system of locating and putting away parts and products. Review Figure 5.1, Inventory movement through a warehouse. List your recommendations in the space provided below.

_____

_____

_____

_____

_____

_____

_____

See page 118 in the back of the book for suggested responses.

M O D U L E

VI

Distribution Inventory Planning and Control

Learning Objectives

After completing this module, you will be able to

- Complete a DRP/MRP problem
- Describe and compare the types of Distribution Inventory Systems
- Discuss the impact of Just-in-Time (JIT) on distribution

DELIVERING PRODUCTS

The physical distribution of products flows through a variety of geographically placed distribution points. The distribution points could include the manufacturing facilities, distribution centers, wholesalers and retailers, or the distribution of goods may flow directly to the customer or through various levels as shown below. Inventory is carried at each location based on criteria such as cost, desired customer-satisfaction level, and efficiency of the distribution operation.

The physical distribution of products must be considered in all types of manufacturing environments (build-to-stock, build-to-order, and assemble-to-order) as well as in wholesale and retail environments.

Following is a diagram that shows how physical distribution and material management fit together to make up the logical flow of goods.

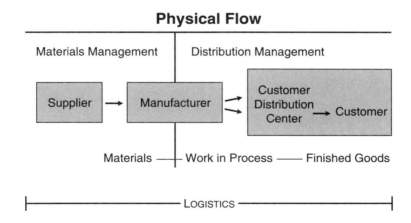

LOGISTICS

Logistics includes the activities of acquiring material (procurement), moving material through the manufacturing environment (manufacturing of products), and distribution (getting the products to, or close to, the final customer).

✓ **Distribution requirements planning** involves meeting customer requirements and receiving and storing goods at the lowest cost possible. In most cases distribution encompasses the process of customer order entry through delivery of the product to the customer.

✓ **Distribution resource planning (DRP)** extends distribution requirements planning into the planning of key resources contained in a distribution system: warehouse space, workforce, money, trucks, freight cars and so on.

✓ **Distribution inventory** includes all inventory anywhere in the distribution system. In most cases, it is finished goods inventory; however, in some cases parts, subassemblies and assemblies can be part of distribution inventory. In all cases this inventory is very expensive; the objective is to manage it by moving it through the distribution system as quickly as possible.

TYPES OF DISTRIBUTION SYSTEMS

Distribution systems are loosely classified as either a push or a pull system.

▶ **PULL SYSTEMS**—In a pull system decisions for replenishment of the inventory are made at the field warehouse. This is in contrast to the centralized decision making in the push systems. The advantage of a pull system is that control is placed with the field management team. The potential disadvantage is the lack of visibility between warehouses, which could result in excess inventory.

▶ **PUSH SYSTEMS**—This pushes the inventory from a central factory out to the warehouse. *Replenishment decisions are made at the manufacturing site.* The advantage to the push system is the economies of scale provided by a central source such as the factory. The disadvantage is the lack of flexibility in responding to local customer requirements.

The most common push system is distribution requirements planning (DRP). This is an MRP-like process using time-phased order point techniques to reflect the demands and planned future orders for all levels of the distribution system.

Forecasting of independent demand, together with actual sales data is exploded through the various levels of distribution. The point of connection between the manufacturing system and the distribution system is the master production schedule (MPS).

In a push system of distribution inventory planning and control, a central control point such as a factory establishes the amount of inventory each distribution center will receive.

This centralized push system is mainly used in situations where the distribution center and the manufacturing center are owned by the same company.

The decision of how much and when to send products is made by the central decision-making department, based on forecasted demand. The subject of forecasting, forecast errors and their impact on inventory, was discussed in Module III.

FORECASTING STOCKKEEPING UNIT (SKU) REQUIREMENTS

The forecast for SKU requirements in a distribution system usually falls into two types: forecast based on aggregate (total) demand and forecast based on allocations.

1. Aggregate forecasts are completed for each distribution center and then summed, to determine the total forecasted demand. This forecasted demand would include the required safety stock to buffer against demand fluctuations.

2. Forecasting by allocation starts with a forecasted total and then allocates a portion of this total to each distribution center.

Irrespective of which forecasting method is used, the impact of change to the original forecast must also be considered. A sample of these changes includes changes in customer and in product demand, lead times, material availability, and unplanned interruptions in the work flow, such as strikes.

As a result of these changes, safety stock must be maintained at a level to ensure that inventory is available when the customers want it. In addition, safety lead time may be used to buffer against fluctuation in demand. This simply involves the expansion of quoted lead time.

Equal Run-Out/Fair Share Quantity Logic

Regardless of how carefully the planning process is carried out, sometimes there is not enough product to be distributed. When this occurs a technique called "fair share" or "equal run-out allocation" may be employed. This method simply attempts to allocate material or parts fairly to each location.

This is a method of allocating scarce products/inventory with the purpose of keeping as many customers happy as possible.

This method is used in a centralized push distribution system to provide inventory to as many distribution centers as possible. The importance of the customer, size of order, and contractual obligations are also considered when determining the equal run-out or fair share quantities.

INTEGRATING DISTRIBUTION AND MANUFACTURING SYSTEMS

The following figure shows a simplified sequence that the distribution system and the master production schedule (MPS) would follow in order to integrate the distribution and manufacturing system.

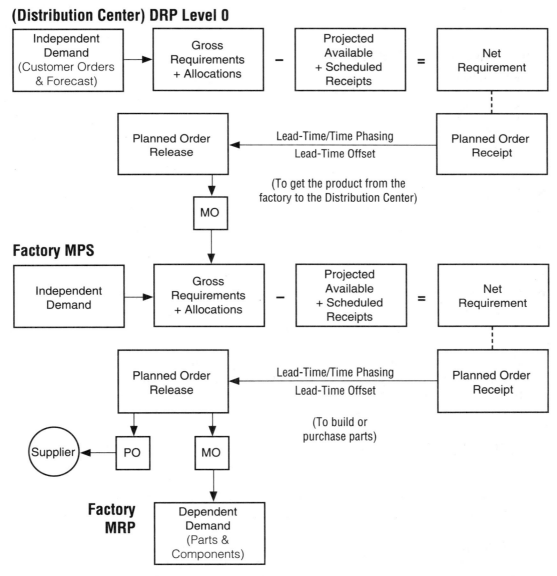

Figure 6.1: Process for Determining Gross-to-Net Requirements

The MPS section of Figure 6.1 is discussed in the following pages.

INTEGRATING DISTRIBUTION AND MANUFACTURING SYSTEMS (continued)

Time-Phased Order Point (TPOP)

TPOP is used in a distribution system to schedule the right item at the right time at the right place and in the right amount. The logic used in the MRP system in used here, as well.

(Distribution Center) DRP Level 0

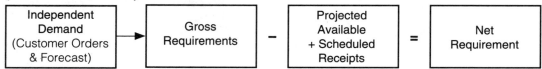

▶ **Independent Demand:** Independent demand comes from sources such as the forecasts, customer orders for end items, as well as repair parts. Independent demand is demand for an end item or service part that is unrelated to the demand for other items. The DRP and MPS contain only independent demand.

▶ **Gross Requirements:** Gross requirements are the total dependent and/or independent requirements for a product or part prior to accounting for the item currently on hand or scheduled to be received.

▶ **Projected Available On-hand Inventory:** On-hand inventory is the quantity that is physically located in stock, and shown in the inventory records as being physically in stock. Periodically, this on-hand inventory is reconciled to the financial inventory (book inventory).

▶ **Scheduled Receipts:** Scheduled receipts are orders already released (opened) either to the distribution center (customer order), manufacturing (production, manufacturing, or shop orders), or to suppliers (purchase orders). Orders released in a prior planning horizon are scheduled to arrive during the current planning horizon.

▶ **Net Requirements:** The net requirements are order amounts that remain after on-hand and scheduled receipts are subtracted from gross requirements.

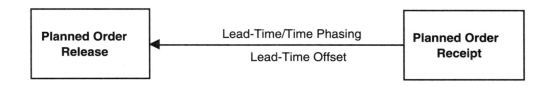

► **Planned Order Receipt:** When there is a net requirement, you must plan to receive an order to satisfy it. If you do not, a material shortage will result. A planned order receipt is the quantity you plan to receive at a future date. Planned order receipts differ from scheduled receipts in that they may change during subsequent planning periods. Scheduled receipts, on the other hand, have been built or are in the process of being built, either by suppliers or internally. Changes to the scheduled receipts are very costly.

► **Lead-Time:** In order to receive an order into the distribution center, you need to determine the amount of time it takes to receive the order from your manufacturing floor or from the supplier. This length of time is called lead-time.

► **Time Phasing/Lead-Time Offsetting:** Time phasing enables you to look into the future in order to plan. (This is better than psychic friends.)

This lead-time offset is established by determining when the item is needed to satisfy a requirement. This allows the MRP system to schedule a planned order receipt in one time period and the planned order release in an earlier time period. The difference between these two dates is the required lead time to make, buy, and/or deliver.

INTEGRATING DISTRIBUTION AND MANUFACTURING SYSTEMS (continued)

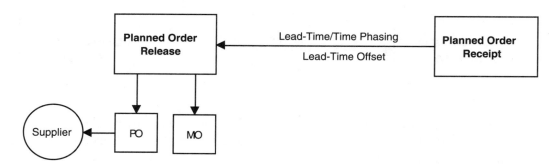

► **Planned Order Release:** A planned order release suggests an order be created, including quantity, release date and due date. It suggests that a purchase order (PO) or manufacturing order (MO) is to be created. Planned orders exist only within the MRP system, and may be changed or deleted by the computer during subsequent MRP processing if conditions change.

The planned order release results in purchase orders, which are given to suppliers, and manufacturing orders, which are sent to the shop floor. In the case of an MO, a planned order release at one level creates a gross requirement at the next level.

MPS Level 0

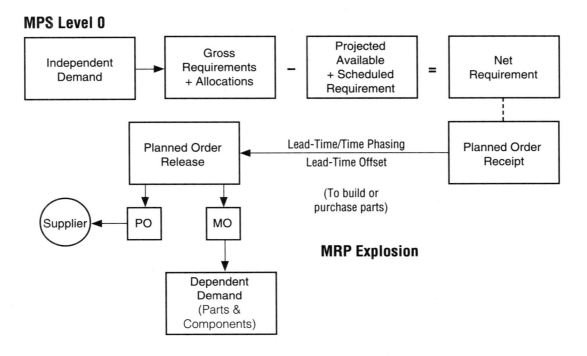

MRP Explosion

▶ **Dependent Demand:** Dependent demand is the demand for all the components required to satisfy the independent demand.

Dependent demand is directly related to or derived from the bill of material (BOM) structure for other items or end products. These demands are calculated, not forecasted. Independent demand is forecasted, and any given item may have both dependent and independent demand. For example, a part may be the component of an assembly and may also be sold as a service part. The MRP represents dependent demand.

EXERCISE 1: Calculations

In this exercise you will build on what you've learned by doing a complete DRP/ MPS/MRP calculation for Product F. The gross requirements have been entered for Product F at the Western and Eastern Region Distribution Centers. Lot sizes, lead times, and projected on-hand balances have been entered. For the following situation, determine the planned order releases. See page 119 in the back of the book for the correct answers.

Product F—Distribution Center (Western Region)

Lot size = 250 Lead-time offset = 3 weeks		Week					
		1	2	3	4	5	6
	Gross Requirements	100	50	200	200	200	200
	Scheduled Receipts			250			
	Projected on-hand = 250						
	Net Requirements						
	Planned order receipt						
	Planned order release						

Product F—Distribution Center (Eastern Region)

Lot size = 300 Lead-time offset = 2 weeks		Week					
		1	2	3	4	5	6
	Gross Requirements	120	120	140	140	160	
	Scheduled Receipts						
	Projected on-hand = 300						
	Net Requirements						
	Planned order receipt						
	Planned order release						

Product F—Factory Finished Goods—MPS

Lot size = 400 Lead-time offset = 1 week		Week					
		1	2	3	4	5	6
	Gross Requirements						
	Scheduled Receipts						
	Projected on-hand = 750						
	Net Requirements						
	Planned order receipt						
	Planned order release						

JUST-IN-TIME IN A DISTRIBUTION ENVIRONMENT

Just-in-Time (JIT) manufacturing evolved from work done in the area of quality control from the early 1950s through the 1980s. JIT programs were influenced by continual process improvements. From a broad view, just-in-time is a philosophy. From a very narrow view, just-in-time means scheduling the right part, at the right place, at the right time.

Total quality control and total quality management have been the driving forces behind the evolution toward JIT.

Just-in-Time is a philosophy that is just as applicable in the distribution and transportation areas as it is in the manufacturing facilities.

In addition to the cost reduction, Just-In-Time principles aid in cost reduction by

- ▶ **Improving Housekeeping:** Housekeeping revolves around removing all items that are not really essential to performing the operation or the job, for example, excess parts, personal items, tools that are not being utilized and defective material. The first step, then, is to clean up the work area, organize the distribution center and terminal, and define who is responsible for keeping that work area clean. The result is better organization and improved visibility and work efficiency.

- ▶ **Reducing Inventory:** By minimizing the amount of inventory in the distribution channel, the overall level of inventory and the related cost to carry the inventory can be reduced. This inventory reduction also reduces lead time and contributes to faster time-to-market. Physical inventories at the distribution center are faster, easier, and more accurate.

- ▶ **Reducing Lead Time:** The reduction in overall distribution lead-time in turn allows for faster deliveries to customers.

- ▶ **Improving Material Handling:** Improved material handling and the subsequent reduction in unplanned downtime also reduce lead-times.

JUST-IN-TIME IN A DISTRIBUTION ENVIRONMENT (continued)

► **Simplifying Processes:** Provides a smooth flow from supplier to customer: Once processes are documented, waste (such as excess inventory, effort, etc.) can be eliminated. This elimination of waste simplifies the process, which in turn allows the product to flow through these processes faster. As products are ordered from the customer, the order can be pulled through the entire supplier/manufacturer/distribution system faster.

Stocking points can be reduced at some of the intermediate locations—not only for the supplier but to the customer, as well.

By using local suppliers, small quantities with faster deliveries can be achieved. Many shippers are using standard-sized reusable containers to cut cost and reduce delivery times. This also makes cycle counts easier and faster. In some cases, the return to the supplier of an empty container is a signal to deliver.

► **Promoting Organizationwide Involvement:** For the types of changes that have been discussed to take place, all functional groups must be involved. JIT is an organizationwide concept, not just a manufacturing responsibility. It is impossible to do JIT supplying if your customers are not doing JIT.

CASE STUDY, PART 3: JADE Inc.

In the last part of the work you did for JADE Inc., you prepared a list of qualitative and quantitative factors the company should consider when locating a new warehouse. The company has now asked you to expand your work. They would like you to prepare a list of cost elements they should include when determining the overall cost of a new distribution system. Note: In your answer, expand on the items covered in this book and include items based on your experience.

_____

_____

_____

_____

_____

_____

_____

_____

_____

Part 2: After considering the total cost of transportation and storage, the percentage of the cost of goods sold, for each item, needs to be considered. However, all costs are still an expense, and any reduction in them has a potential positive impact on profit, assuming customer satisfaction is not jeopardized.

Now list some of the ways distribution costs may be reduced:

- _____

- _____

- _____

See page 120 in the back of this book for suggested answers.

CASE STUDY, PART 4: JADE Inc.

In your last presentation to the executives of JADE Inc., you recommended that your contract be extended in order to do a study on the various types of transportation methods they should use in their new distribution system.

They accepted your proposal, and asked you to list the advantages and disadvantages of each method using the following chart. Note: In your answer, expand on the items covered in this book and include items based on your experience.

Method of Transportation	Advantages	Disadvantages
Air		
Water		
Railroad		
Pipeline		
Road vehicle		

See page 121 in the back of the book for suggested answers.

EXERCISE 2: *Choose the Correct Answer*

Answer the following questions. See page 119 in the back of the book for the correct answers.

1. List the types of Distribution Inventory Systems.

_____

_____

2. Which of the following statements best describes Distribution Resource Planning?

   I. Same as Distribution Requirement Planning
   II. Uses TPOP
   III. In addition to product distribution, deals with facilities, people, trucks, etc.

   A. I and II
   B. III only
   C. II and III

3. Which of the following statements best describes Distribution Requirements Planning?

   I. Uses TPOP
   II. Uses MRP Logic
   III. Is the same as CRP

   A. III only
   B. II and III
   C. I and II
   D. All of the above

4. Which of the following statements describes a push system?

   I. A system of replenishing field warehouse inventories
   II. Uses decentralized decision making
   III. Is included in EOQ

   A. I only
   B. II and III
   C. All of the above

5. In allocating inventories to warehouses, the equal run-out method accomplishes the following:

   A. An equal supply at each location
   B. The accuracy of the cycle count
   C. Minimized inventory investment
   D. Maximum production efficiency

NOTE TO THE READER

In this book we've explored the competitive issues facing business today, and you've been introduced to the theory, tools and techniques that can make inventory management possible. We've discussed the objectives and policies, inventory systems, tools and techniques, physical inventory control, and you've had an opportunity to practice using many tools. At this point you have the knowledge and skills necessary to launch and/or support your own continual improvement process. Now, what can you do each day to increase your net worth and make yourself more marketable in the manufacturing arena?

As the future unfolds in front of us and we bring new products to market faster and faster, I'm convinced that the manufacturing formulas presented in this book will play a major role. But the most important role will be played by the portion of the formula that focuses on improving the forecasting process and the subsequent reduction in the forecast error. It is my hope that you will use this formula and the other tools successfully on the job, that you will teach others, and that as a result we will reach the critical mass required to manufacture on an environmentally safe, global basis. Forecasting and Scheduling is the topic of my next book.

Good Luck.

Answers to Exercises

Module I Answers

EXERCISE 1: Match Game (page 11)

1. e **2.** c **3.** d **4.** g **5.** a **6.** f **7.** b

EXERCISE 2: Fill In the Blanks (page 12)

1. a. Maximize customer service
   b. Maximize efficiency of people and machines
   c. Minimize inventory investment
   d. Maximize profit

2. a. Raw material
   b. Work-in-process
   c. Finished goods
   d. Distribution inventory
   e. Maintenance, repair and operating supplies

Module II Answers

EXERCISE 1: Calculations (page 19)

Order point 1 = 4,000 (2,000 × 2 weeks) + 200 = 4,200

Order point 2 = 4,200 + 6,000 (3 × 2,000) = 10,200

EXERCISE 2: Choose the Correct Answer (page 26)

1. D **2.** D **3.** D **4.** B **5.** B **6.** A

Module III Answers

EXERCISE 1: Calculations (page 48)

1. Your answers should look like this:

A. Units: $EOQ = \sqrt{\dfrac{2US}{IC}} = \sqrt{\dfrac{2 \times 5,500 \times 100}{0.2 \times 10}}, \sqrt{550,000}$

EOQ = 741.62

B. \$: $EOQ = \sqrt{\dfrac{2AS}{1}} = \sqrt{\dfrac{2 \times \$60,000 \times 100}{0.2}}, \sqrt{\$60,000,000}$

EOQ = \$7,745.96

2. Your completed table should look like the one below.

Time Period	Forecast	Sales	Forecast Error	Forecast Error^2 (squared)
1	500	600	100	10,000
2	500	500	0	0
3	500	400	−100	10,000
4	500	450	−50	2,500
5	500	700	200	40,000
6	500	600	100	10,000
7	500	550	50	2,500
8	500	500	0	0
9	500	350	−150	22,500
10	500	450	50	2,500
Total	**5,000**	**5,100**		**100,000**

A. Standard Deviation:

$$\frac{100,000}{10} = 10,000$$

$$\sqrt{10,000} = 100$$

B. $\text{MAD} = \dfrac{800}{10} = 80 \times 1.25 = 100$

EXERCISE 2: Fill In the Blanks (page 50)

Part A. Your chart should look like this:

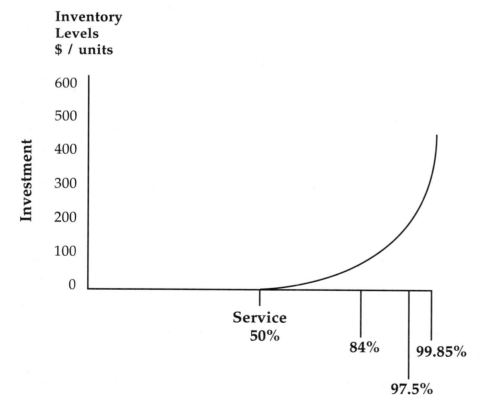

Inventory Levels $ / units

Part B. 600 (6 × 100—one standard deviation)

EXERCISE 3: Choose the Correct Answer (page 51)

1. D **2.** D **3.** B (not a type of lot sizing) **4.** D **5.** C

Module IV Answers

EXERCISE 2: Calculating Ratios (page 65)

Does your completed table look like this?

Key Financial Ratios
(rounded to the nearest one-hundredths)

NAME	METHOD OF CALCULATION	ANSWERS	
		Prior Year	Current Year
Liquidity			
Current Ratio	$\dfrac{\text{Current Assets}}{\text{Current Liabilities}}$	2.05	1.45
Quick Ratio	$\dfrac{\text{Cash + Receivables}}{\text{Current Liabilities}}$	1.09	.43
Days Sales Outstanding (DSO)	$\dfrac{\text{Receivables} \times 365}{\text{Net Sales}}$	29.2	45.6
Inventory Turnover	$\dfrac{\text{Cost of Goods Sold}}{\text{Inventory}}$	6.19	1.26
Leverage			
Debt-to-Equity	$\dfrac{\text{Total Liabilites}}{\text{Equity}}$	.99	1.84
Profitability			
Return on Equity	$\dfrac{\text{Net Income}}{\text{Equity}}$	.33	.39
Return on Assets	$\dfrac{\text{Net Income}}{\text{Total Assets}}$	.17	.14

EXERCISE 3: Valuing Inventory (page 74)

LIFO		Cost of sales	Inventory Value
June	2000 × 4.50 =	$ 9,000	
May	1000 × 4.50 =	4,500	
April	1000 × 4.40 =	4,400	
April	500 × 4.40		$ 2,200
March	1000 × 4.20		4,200
February	2000 × 4.20		8,400
January	1000 × 4.00		4,000
		$17,900	**$18,800**

FIFO		Cost of sales	Inventory Value
January	1000 × 4.00 =	$ 4,000	
February	2000 × 4.20 =	8,400	
March	1000 × 4.20 =	4,200	
April	1500 × 4.40		$ 6,600
May	1000 × 4.50		4,500
June	2000 × 4.50		9,000
		$16,600	**$20,100**

Standard Cost:

Total purchases 8,500 units

$4.40 × 4000 = $17,600 – Cost of Sales

$4.40 × 4500 = $19,800 – Inventory Value

Replacement Cost (inventory):

$4.65 × 4500 = $20,925

MODULE IV ANSWERS (continued)

EXERCISE 4: Choose the Correct Answer (page 75)

1. C   **2.** C   **3.** A

Module V Answers

EXERCISE 1: Fill In the Charts (page 83)

1. Your completed chart should look like the one below.

ABC Analysis Based on Annual Dollar Volume
Annual Dollar Volume Percentages

	1	2	3	4
Item	Unit Cost	Annual Usage (units)	Anual Usage (dollars)	% of Total Dollar Usage
1	$ 4.00	1,250	$ 5,000	.8
2	2.50	1,500	3,750	.6
3	3.00	10,000	30,000	4.6
4	36.00	4,000	144,000	22.0
5	31.00	12,500	387,500	59.0
6	.517	8,000	4,136	.6
7	25.00	1,480	37,000	5.6
8	325.00	100	32,500	5.0
9	8.00	625	5,000	.8
10	6.00	1,000	6,000	1.0
		Total	$654,886	100%

2. The answers ranked from the highest annual usage to the lowest.

Item	Annual Usage (dollars)	% of Total	Cumulative %	Classification
	1	2	3	4
5	387,500	59.0	59.0	A
4	144,000	22.0	81.0	A
7	37,000	5.6	86.6	B
8	32,500	5.0	91.6	B
3	30,000	4.6	96.2	B
10	6,000	1.0	97.2	C
1	5,000	.8	98.0	C
9	5,000	.8	98.8	C
6	4,136	.6	99.4	C
2	3,750	.6	100.0	C

CASE STUDY, PART 1: JADE Inc. (page 86)

Do your answers include this information?

1. Quantitative costs include

- Transportation in and out
- Cost of land and construction
- Existing buildings and their related costs
- City, county and state taxes and licenses
- Cost of living and related salaries

2. Qualitative costs include

- Availability of trained people
- Facilities such as schools, hospitals, etc.
- City, county and state regulations
- Environmental regulations
- Unions

MODULE V ANSWERS (continued)

CASE STUDY, PART 2: JADE Inc. (page 89)

Some of your recommendations might include the following:

- Locate fast-moving items close to the receiving and shipping docks.

- Place slow-moving items in remote areas of the warehouse.

- Store small, high-value items in a caged (locked) area.

- Group similar-sized items together—bulk items in a bulk area, smaller packages on shelves, and specialty items in approved containers. (NOTE: Gases and toxic material must be properly stored according to government regulations.)

- Any stock used by warehouse operations should be segregated from stock being stored.

EXERCISE 2: Choose the Correct Answer (page 88)

1 C

2. Major warehouse activities include

   Receiving

   Storing

   Identifying

   Picking

   Packaging

   Shipping

3. Floating location

   Fixed location

4. D

Module VI Answers

EXERCISE 1: Calculations (page 102)

The planned order releases should look like this:

Product F—Distribution Center (Western Region)

		Week					
		1	**2**	**3**	**4**	**5**	**6**
Lot size = 250 Lead-time offset = 3 weeks	Gross Requirements	100	50	200	200	200	200
	Scheduled Receipts			250			
	Projected on-hand = 250	150	100	150	200	0	50
	Net Requirements				−50		−200
	Planned order receipt				250		250
	Planned order release	250		250			

Product F—Distribution Center (Eastern Region)

		Week					
		1	**2**	**3**	**4**	**5**	**6**
Lot size = 300 Lead-time offset = 2 weeks	Gross Requirements	120	120	140	140	160	
	Scheduled Receipts						
	Projected on-hand = 300	180	60	220	80	220	220
	Net Requirements			−80		−80	
	Planned order receipt			300		300	
	Planned order release	300		300			

Product F—Factory Finished Goods—MPS

		Week					
		1	**2**	**3**	**4**	**5**	**6**
Lot size = 400 Lead-time offset = 1 week	Gross Requirements	550		550			
	Scheduled Receipts						
	Projected on-hand = 750	200	200	50	50	50	50
	Net Requirements			−350			
	Planned order receipt			400			
	Planned order release		400				

EXERCISE 2: Choose the Correct Answer (page 107)

1. Push, Pull **2.** B **3.** C **4.** A **5.** A

MODULE VI ANSWERS (continued)

CASE STUDY, PART 3: JADE Inc. (page 105)

A. Your list of cost elements should include the following:

- Initial Transportation
  - —Air
  - —Water
  - —Railroad
  - —Pipeline
  - —Roadway
- Pickup and delivery
- Cost of building, renting and maintaining the terminals, warehouses, and distribution centers
- Storing/carrying costs
- Insurance
- Material handling costs
- Licenses
- Freight management and administration
- Import/Export

B. Some of the ways distribution costs my be reduced are

- Locating a local supplier
- Drop shipping directly to the customer
- Using reusable containers
- Minimizing returns
- Reducing data-entry time through bar coding
- Reducing the amount of inventory in the pipeline
- Reducing billing and collection costs
- Properly utilizing space

CASE STUDY PART 4: JADE Inc. (page 106)

Your chart should look similar to this.

Method of Transportation	Advantages	Disadvantages
Air	• Fastest to customer • May be appropriate for small, expensive items	• Expensive • Limit to size and quantity
Water	• No limit to size and quantity • Cost may be less	• Slowest method • Limited mobility
Railroad	• Capable of large volumes and sizes • Cost per unit is relatively low	• Limited mobility • Limited facilities
Pipeline	• Over time, cost per unit is reduced	• Limited application
Road vehicle	• Very mobile • Good for short distance solutions	• High cost of maintenance • Expensive per unit

NOTES

NOTES

Now Available From

CRISP PUBLICATIONS

Books•Videos•CD-ROMs•Computer-Based Training Products

If you enjoyed this book, we have great news for you. There are over 200 books available in the *50-Minute*™ Series. To request a free full-line catalog, contact your local distributor or Crisp Publications, Inc., 1200 Hamilton Court, Menlo Park, CA 94025. Our toll-free number is 800-442-7477. Visit our website at: www.crisplearning.com.

Subject Areas Include:

Management

Human Resources

Communication Skills

Personal Development

Marketing/Sales

Organizational Development

Customer Service/Quality

Computer Skills

Small Business and Entrepreneurship

Adult Literacy and Learning

Life Planning and Retirement

CRISP WORLDWIDE DISTRIBUTION

English language books are distributed worldwide. Major international distributors include:

ASIA/PACIFIC

Australia/New Zealand: In Learning, PO Box 1051, Springwood QLD, Brisbane, Australia 4127   Tel: 61-7-3-841-2286, Facsimile: 61-7-3-841-1580
ATTN: Messrs. Gordon

Philippines: National Book Store Inc., Quad Alpha Centrum Bldg, 125 Pioneer Street, Mandaluyong, Metro Manila, Philippines   Tel: 632-631-8051, Facsimile: 632-631-5016

Singapore, Malaysia, Brunei, Indonesia: Times Book Shops. Direct sales HQ: STP Distributors, Pasir Panjang Distrientre, Block 1 #03-01A, Pasir Panjang Rd, Singapore 118480   Tel: 65-2767626, Facsimile: 65-2767119

Japan: Phoenix Associates Co., Ltd., Mizuho Bldng, 3-F, 2-12-2, Kami Osaki, Shinagawa-Ku, Tokyo 141   Tel: 81-33-443-7231, Facsimile: 81-33-443-7640
ATTN: Mr. Peter Owans

CANADA

Reid Publishing, Ltd., Box 69559, 60 Briarwood Avenue, Port Credit, Ontario, Canada L5G 3N6 Tel: (905) 842-4428, Facsimile: (905) 842-9327
ATTN: Mr. Steve Connolly/Mr. Jerry McNabb

Trade Book Stores: Raincoast Books, 8680 Cambie Street, Vancouver, B.C., V6P 6M9 Tel: (604) 323-7100, Facsimile: (604) 323-2600   ATTN: Order Desk

EUROPEAN UNION

England: Flex Training, Ltd., 9-15 Hitchin Street, Baldock, Hertfordshire, SG7 6A, England Tel: 44-1-46-289-6000, Facsimile: 44-1-46-289-2417
ATTN: Mr. David Willetts

INDIA

Multi-Media HRD, Pvt., Ltd., National House, Tulloch Road, Appolo Bunder, Bombay, India 400-039   Tel: 91-22-204-2281, Facsimile: 91-22-283-6478
ATTN: Messrs. Aggarwal

SOUTH AMERICA

Mexico: Grupo Editorial Iberoamerica, Nebraska 199, Col. Napoles, 03810 Mexico, D.F. Tel: 525-523-0994, Facsimile: 525-543-1173   ATTN: Señor Nicholas Grepe

SOUTH AFRICA

Alternative Books, PO Box 1345, Ferndale 2160, South Africa
Tel: 27-11-792-7730, Facsimile: 27-11-792-7787   ATTN: Mr. Vernon de Haas